BROOKLANDS COLLEGE LIBRARY
CHURCH ROAD, ASHFORD, MIDDLESEX TW15 2XD
Tel: (01784) 248666

This item must be returned on or before the last date
entered below. Subject to certain conditions, the loan
period may be extended upon application to the Librarian

AUTHOR ..... MASTERS

TITLE ..... Working in sport

CLASSIFICATION NO. ..... MB

ACCESSION NO. 100186

If you want to know how . . .

How to Write a Great CV
*Discover what interviewers are looking for, focus on your
strengths and perfect your presentation*

Passing Psychometric Tests
Know what to expect and get the job you want

Pass that Interview
Your step-by-step guide to coming out on top

Get That Job!
*The complete, thorough, hands-on guide to the whole
recruitment and selection process – for ambitious
graduates in early career*

howtobooks

Please send for a free copy of the latest catalogue:

How To Books
Spring Hill House, Spring Hill Road,
Begbroke, Oxford OX5 1RX, United Kingdom
Tel: (01865) 375794. Fax: (01865) 379162.
email: info@howtobooks.co.uk
www.howtobooks.co.uk

Working in sport

How to find a sports related job in the UK or abroad

2nd edition

James Masters

howtobooks

Published by How To Books Ltd,
Spring Hill House, Spring Hill Road,
Begbroke, Oxford OX5 1RX, United Kingdom
Tel: (01865) 375794. Fax: (01865) 379162
email: info@howtobooks.co.uk
www.howtobooks.co.uk

British Library Cataloguing in Publication Data
A catalogue record for this book is available from the British Library

ISBN: 978 1 84528 176 2

Cover design by Baseline Arts Ltd, Oxford
Produced for How To Books by Deer Park Productions, Tavistock
Typeset by PDQ Typesetting Ltd, Staffordshire
Printed and bound by Cromwell Press Ltd., Trowbridge, Wiltshire

NOTE: The material contained in this book is set out in good faith for general
guidance and no liability can be accepted for loss or expense incurred as a
result of relying in particular circumstances on statements made in the book.
Laws and regulations are complex and liable to change, and readers should
check the current position with the relevant authorities before making
personal arrangements.

Contents

List of Illustrations

Foreword

James first coached me at athletics when I was a 14-year-old. Initially I was a club standard distance runner, but with his coaching I not only became more competent at this, but also became a North of England standard pole vaulter and representative 400 metre hurdler.

James then encouraged me to develop my all round ability which paid dividends later when I quit athletics. Initially we worked at javelin, high jump and then the rest of the decathlon events. By the time I was 19 years old I was ranked as the number one Junior Decathlete (using junior implements) in Great Britain.

Unfortunately I stopped growing after this, remaining 1.70m, which was much too small to succeed at national senior decathlon level. Fortunately, however, our all-round training enabled me to switch sports.

Although I didn't attend the school that James taught at, he arranged for me to go on one of their annual ski trips. I got the bug!

After one more skiing holiday I approached the British Ski Federation to try out as a ski jumper, and made their squad. I attended a summer training squad in Kandersteg, Switzerland, where I beat Eddie Edwards, in dry slope jumps, on several occasions. I would have pursued this option and probably have successfully represented GB in numerous championships had it not been for financial reasons.

However, the main lesson learned was that the type of training and advice that James gave me was absolutely vital in my development. I have also witnessed him being equally invaluable to other sportsmen. I am certain that the advice he gives in his book will be extremely useful to you too.

Simon Mitchell
Ex GB number one Junior Decathlete,
GB Ski Jump and Bobsleigh Squads

Preface

This is the second edition of this book and, although the first edition was generally well received and critically acclaimed, I think this version is much improved.

Many things have happened since the first book. I wrote then that there were many jobs advertised on the internet, but that the majority advertised in the UK were contained in magazines. The internet was mainly prevalent in the USA as the world wide web wasn't as well developed in this country. That has now been turned on its head since the explosion of broadband. The vast majority of the work listed in Chapter 4 for the UK is now sourced from the internet.

There are several other updates in this edition, but rather than list them here I suggest you continue reading and discover these for yourself. I hope that you find this book useful.

The idea for this series of books was born after innumerable members of my coaching groups and pupils at the school in which I was Head of PE asked me for advice. I then realised that there was a huge need for this resource in libraries. So here it is, the second edition.

If it had been around when I was making major decisions on leaving school/college, I know it would have changed my life. I hope that it helps to shape your choices.

Good luck.

ACKNOWLEDGEMENTS

As in the previous edition it would not have been possible to write this book without the invaluable assistance of the people listed below. If I have missed anybody from this list, I apologise, it wasn't intentional.

The following people and organisations have given invaluable assistance in compiling this book. My sincere thanks go to them, as without their help this book would be far less interesting.

Steven Armstrong, Steve Atkinson, Gareth Couzens, Steve Dix, Jim Eason, Gary Ferguson, Karen Flint, Simon Flint, Ollie Haum, Steve Huggins, Ian Jefferson, John Little, Ian McGuckin, Simon Mitchell, Kevin Rudd, plus Andy Bell of Soccer Coach USA, Stuart Dowsett of Brussels Barbarians Rugby Club, John Gaylard and *Horse and Hound* magazine, David Holmes at British Dressage, Martin Hudson of P.G.L., Mark Warner Ltd, *Rugby World* magazine, Dave Sturdy and *FourFourTwo* magazine, David Wear the Estate Manager at Beamish Open Air Museum.

Although every effort has been made to ensure that this book is as accurate and up to date as is possible, no liability can be accepted by the author or publisher. Things change. It is inevitable that during the lifetime of this book some of the data will become outdated and some errors or omissions will become evident. Readers should satisfy themselves as to the book's accuracy before relying on it. No liability can be accepted by the author or publisher for disappointment, loss, negligence or other damage caused by relying solely on the information that this book contains, nor in the event of bankruptcy, liquidation or cessation of trade of any company, individual or firm.

James Masters

(1)

Making the Most of Your Skills

Alan Shearer recently retired from football and, when asked if he had any regrets about his career, he publicly stated that he had none. His dream had been to play professional football for Newcastle United, and he had lived his dream.

Not many people can say that.

I'm sure that 99 per cent of youngsters dream about being rich and famous one day. Some dream about being a film star or a successful pop singer. For others the fantasy is of scoring the winning goal at Wembley, or taking the trophy at Wimbledon or the US Masters. Unfortunately this is normally as far as it gets, because only one person each year can achieve this dream out of the millions, *literally* millions, who have dreamt it.

PURSUING YOUR DREAM

That doesn't mean, however, that it is not worth trying to pursue your fantasy. Somebody, like Shearer, has got to achieve it, but you cannot live life in a dream world. A lot of reality has got to be mixed with a little fantasy. You have got to be *exceptionally* talented, with nerves of steel and a will to work extremely hard to go this far. Most people lack at least one of these qualities. Even the people who possess all of them still find themselves in an incredibly large pool of very talented people.

Fortunately, though, this doesn't have to be the end of your sporting dream. There are still numerous other opportunities, besides being a pro sportsman, that would enable you to make a career out of your sport, or at least to simply enjoy it while it lasts.

In the first edition of this book I reported that the Central Council for Physical Recreation (CCPR) estimated there to be nearly half a million people making their living out of working in sport in Britain. This number has now risen dramatically.

In 2005 it was estimated that 40,000 people worked in sport in Scotland alone. The leisure industry continues to be a huge growth area for the employment of British citizens at home and an increasing number working abroad. If you add the number of these foreign workers to our national employment figures then the amount of Brits working in some form of sporting capacity is now astronomical.

Mark Warner Ltd is one of the leaders in the provision of 'active' holidays in Britain. Each year they employ over 1,500 staff to work in some of Europe's top ski resorts and locations around the Mediterranean and Aegean, and there are many other big employers in this field including Club Med, Crystal Holidays, First Choice, PGL, etc, all of whose contact information can be found in Chapter 9.

There are sports related jobs out there for all standards of playing and coaching ability, as well as all levels of academic achievement. If you are determined enough, with the ability to match, you too could be working in sport, *soon*.

MAKING THE RIGHT MOVE

Would you enjoy it?

Working in sport and enjoying playing it are not one and the same. You often have to work long, unsociable hours coaching other people to compete in the sport that you love. Worse still, you could spend all day cleaning and preparing the equipment or playing area for others to use. Would you enjoy it?

Are you ready and qualified for it?

Don't forget that many other people also want to work in sport. Hundreds of applications are regularly received by employers for these jobs, especially in our bigger cities. To increase your chances of success you may need to move away from home or take extra academic qualifications. Are you prepared to do this?

If you can answer yes to any of the above questions, and have not been put off by the realities of the situation, then maybe this *is* the right move for you. However, if you think that you can just walk into the ideal job straight after leaving school or college, you are most likely to join the long list of disappointed dreamers.

ASSESSING WHETHER THIS MOVE IS RIGHT FOR YOU

1. Examine the flowchart in Figure 1.

2. Find the category in which you would like to find employment.

3. Read the relevant sections in the chapters indicated.

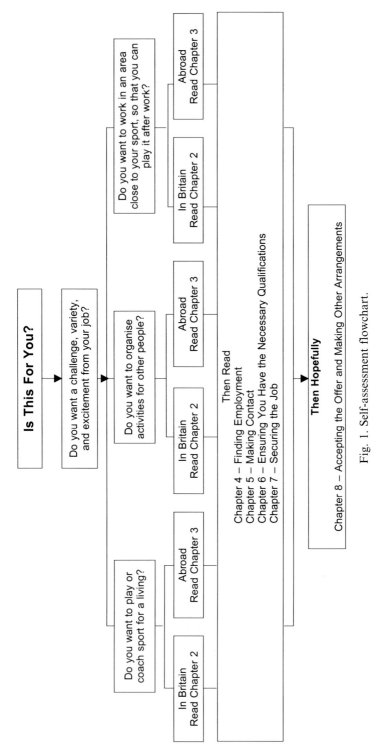

Is This For You?

Do you want a challenge, variety, and excitement from your job?

Do you want to play or coach sport for a living?

Do you want to organise activities for other people?

Do you want to work in an area close to your sport, so that you can play it after work?

In Britain Read Chapter 2

Abroad Read Chapter 3

In Britain Read Chapter 2

Abroad Read Chapter 3

In Britain Read Chapter 2

Abroad Read Chapter 3

Then Read

Chapter 4 – Finding Employment
Chapter 5 – Making Contact
Chapter 6 – Ensuring You Have the Necessary Qualifications
Chapter 7 – Securing the Job

Then Hopefully

Chapter 8 – Accepting the Offer and Making Other Arrangements

Fig. 1. Self-assessment flowchart.

If you are still determined to work in sport, in whatever capacity, it is worth weighing up the pros and cons of this option in Figure 2.

PROS	CONS
◆ Varied workload.	◆ Not a steady 9 to 5 job.
◆ Healthy lifestyle.	◆ Will probably have to work much harder than in an office.
◆ Not boring and repetitive.	◆ May have to work long and irregular hours.
◆ Often gives opportunities to travel.	◆ May have to be away from home frequently.
◆ On site to compete at your own sport.	◆ Often too tired to compete after work.
◆ You get to meet many interesting people.	◆ You may also have to work with people that you don't like.
◆ Satisfaction from achieving something worthwhile.	◆ Often under pressure to resolve tricky situations.
◆ On site to train for your own sport.	◆ After working all day at this site, you may not feel motivated to train there.

Fig. 2. Weighing up the pros and cons.

Still undeterred? Then the following suggestions will help you in your quest.

IMPROVING YOUR CHANCES

Chapter 6, Ensuring You Have the Necessary Qualifications, will tell you what employers require from you. Many jobs need some sort of formal qualifications, so if you don't have the necessary certificates and diplomas you have three choices:

1. Set about acquiring them.
2. Look for a job more suited to your ability.
3. Still apply, hoping that you have other qualities they might be looking for.

Whatever your level of academic qualifications, you can still improve your chances by acquiring some easily obtained skills and experience. The examples below should always be included in your CV or on the application form when applying for work.

- aptitude for car maintenance;
- coaching awards;
- computer literacy;
- council self-help scheme;
- DIY ability;
- driving licence;
- first aid certificate;
- language skills;
- life-saving awards;
- musical ability;
- part-time work;
- sports certificates, awards and trophies;
- scouting;
- typing certificates or expertise;
- voluntary work;
- working for a charity, a youth club, or in a crèche.

I am sure there are many others that haven't been thought of, so don't forget, always include any experience you have gained that you think is relevant to the job for which you are applying. All inclusions will improve your profile and might just give you the edge in interviews. If you don't find the more academic qualifications particularly easy you can still impress prospective employers by gaining some practical qualifications and experience. Adverts for these, and many other courses, regularly appear in your local newspapers. Alternatively you can pop down to your local community college for a prospectus of their courses, as many of these will be based there, and if not they will probably point you in the direction of the course you are looking for.

The basic level certificate is normally quite easy to achieve and within everyone's reach.

Thinking of everything

When applying for a job make sure that you put all of your skills down on your application form. For example, if the work that you are applying for is in England it might not seem relevant to tell the employer that you speak Japanese. However, that company might have a group of Japanese businessmen visiting them during the summer and your ability to communicate with them might give you the edge over other applicants.

An ability to use a computer is always worth mentioning, even if you can do little more than type letters on it. It shows that you are not scared of using one, and that you are likely to be easily trained to do more than you are presently capable of.

Likewise if you are skilful at woodwork, metalwork, needlecraft or other practical skills, mention them. They could be something that the employer is looking for, or could be an indication of your ability to learn another skill. Don't forget that employers don't generally expect you just to start work immediately with all the required skills in place, and will invariably train you up to the standard they require.

Gaining experience

If you don't have any certificates or skills there are other things that impress employers and you mustn't be shy of using them. 'The University of Life' often gives you the *experience* that companies are looking for and many employers place as much importance on this as on the qualifications you might also have gained.

Simply asking at the local hospital or charity if you could do some voluntary work will often lead to a very impressive inclusion in your CV. Libraries are a good source of information if you need to find out about these. *Yellow Pages* can also be useful. Well over 100 different addresses and telephone numbers of various charities are contained in most directories.

Don't forget that working for somebody is only part of the advantage to you. Not only do you gain the experience of the employment to put on your CV, but also, if you have done well at this job, you should get a valuable reference from your employer.

Being given references

Strictly speaking a reference is written confidentially and sent privately to your prospective employer. If you are personally given a written citation from your employer it is called a testimonial. However, over the years these terms seem to have been confused, so it is worth checking which of the two is required by the company to which you are applying.

The following points regarding references and testimonials should be observed.

◆ Any references supplied to the employer should be suitable for the job. A reference regarding your experience and expertise as a joiner might be of little value if you are applying to be a bus driver, but it does show your employability, punctuality, reliability and honesty.

◆ If you haven't had a previous job then a reference or testimonial from your head teacher or principal, schoolteacher, Scout leader, vicar or even a friend could be supplied. They *must* emphasise the strong points of your character.

◆ *All* references and testimonials should be typed, on suitably headed paper. Something scribbled on a scrap of paper not only reflects poorly on you, but could also make the employer suspect that it is a forgery.

◆ *Any* references and testimonials are as valuable to you as academic qualifications. In both cases, keep them safe and in good condition. You will probably use them over and over again. If they look scruffy your interviewer will probably suspect that your standard of work will also lack care and attention.

SELF-ASSESSMENT EXERCISE

1. Is employment in sport right for you? Can you cope with the disadvantages *as well as* the advantages? Remember it is not a regular 9 to 5 job.

2. Are you fit enough to cope with the workload? Don't forget that it will be physically more demanding than sitting behind a desk and the hours may be longer.

3. As this type of work is much sought after you may not be able to get a job close to home. Are you prepared to move anywhere in Britain or abroad?

4. Are you resilient enough to deal with awkward and obnoxious people? Don't forget that working in sport is a 'people' thing.

5. Can you work under pressure? You might sometimes be required to work late to finish a project and also work to a tight deadline.

6. Would you prefer to work abroad? Do you know which country you prefer? Do you know anything about the country? Are you prepared to learn the language?

7. Has the work got to be on a long-term contract? Do you mind temporary work?

8. Have you got the necessary experience and qualifications for this job and, if not, are you prepared to work to get them?

$$\bigodot\ 2$$

Discovering the Opportunities in Britain

PLAYING THE GAME

When you are younger it is quite natural to wonder what you will do when you leave school. It is not normal, however, to dream of becoming a greenkeeper, or a sports centre manager or even a coach in your favourite sport. The fantasy is nearly always of playing for your local professional team, or if even more ambitious of representing Great Britain at a World Cup or Olympic Games.

Most children would play for their local team just for the love of it, regardless of the prestige, the adoration of the fans and the excitement. Money would not be an issue.

A spin-off, though, could be that by fulfilling their dreams they might also have carved out a very lucrative career.

Playing for gold

The kind of money that top soccer players earn is well documented. Recently Thierry Henry signed a new contract with Arsenal which allegedly now earns him £130k a week! Unfortunately, though, not all sports have competitors who earn as much as professional footballers, *but some earn even more!*

The *Sunday Times* produces a 'Rich List' every year and it is worth noting that in 2005 the richest people in Britain were not sportsmen, but were in industry, retail and property. So if your intention is merely to become extremely wealthy maybe that is where you should set your sights.

Several sportsmen did, however, make the top 1,000 on this list, but none made the top 300.

Not all of the fortune amassed by these fortunate sportsmen was purely through wages, though. Much of their wealth was increased by advertising deals, sponsorship and wise investments.

The top earners

The richest sportsman, Formula One driver Eddie Irvine, made 301st on the list, but much of his reported £153m was accrued through property and advertising deals, as well as his motor racing earnings.

Second richest sportsman on the list was footballer David Beckham, but only overall 654th . He possesses a reported £75m although some of this was earned by his wife, Victoria.

The next British sportsmen on the list were also soccer players: Michael Owen (£30 million) and Robbie Fowler, whose investment in property is credited for much of his income.

Formula One driver Jenson Button has numerous sponsorship deals as well as a large salary. This ranks him fifth in the sporting riches, with £20 million.

Other sports that put their players high on this list were:

◆ Tennis, with Tim Henman amassing a £14 million fortune.

◆ Basketball, through Michael Olowokandi, who was raised in Britain but is a star with American basketball team Minnesota Timberwolves. His four-year contract is worth £10.1 million.

◆ Rugby through Jonny Wilkinson who is reportedly worth £8 million.

◆ Golf, courtesy of Ryder Cup star Luke Donald, 27, with a career wealth of £5 million.

So you can see that whatever your sport there is potential to be a huge earner if you can make it to the top of the tree.

Football riches

Although other sports do produce very rich participants, overall by far the richest sportspeople come from soccer. According to The Professional Footballers' Association (2006) in the previous season in Britain £786 million in wages was paid to 2,347 professional footballers. That's roughly £335,000 per player. Obviously the Premiership players earn vastly more than the players in lower divisions, but nevertheless, the lower paid players can still live very comfortably on this wage.

According to a survey by *The Independent* and the Professional Footballers' Association, Premiership footballers in Britain currently earn an average of £676,000 per year. Championship players earn an average salary of £195,750, League One players £67,850 and League Two £49,600.

Competing with foreign players
Unfortunately, though, it is becoming increasingly difficult for British players to achieve the top wages in football as the Premiership is flooded with more and more foreign players. Last season both Chelsea and Arsenal, on more than one occasion, turned out teams without a single British player on the field. Even their managers are imports!

This situation is by no means unusual. The *Times* also reported in their most recent survey that 187 foreigners from 50 different countries played in the Premiership.

This may be good for the standard of the game, but it leaves fewer jobs to go round for our home grown talent. It is also becoming increasingly hard to gain a place in our lower division teams, with more and more foreign nationals playing there. Even some of our second division teams now boast Brazilian and Argentinian players.

Going abroad or staying in the UK
This means that many of our own better players need to move abroad to increase their earning potential. The top two British earners on the *Times'* Rich List both played in Spain.

Due to the influx of foreign players in our game, many of our top footballers who don't go abroad are relegated to being substitutes, playing in the reserves or even in the lower divisions.

Nevertheless, as shown above, a decent living wage can still be earned. Even semi-professional players in the Conference or Northern League can earn more than £200 per week and, of course, this can be topped up by money earned through their other sidelines.

Getting into soccer
Getting into paid employment in soccer is not easy though. The Professional Footballers' Association currently has 4,000 members, and although this figure seems quite high, it is absolutely tiny in comparison with the number of 'applicants' rejected. The failure rate in football is exceptionally high.

Almost every player gets into football by being discovered, rather than applying. Usually they are spotted whilst playing for a minor team and then approached by a scout or someone from the management team of a bigger and wealthier club. If the player they are interested in is still at school they will approach the parents or head teacher. If the player is older they will be approached through their club and invited to attend either a trial or training sessions, where they can be assessed.

Some players *have* written to non-Football League clubs, been offered trials and later been taken on as semi-professionals, but this is rare.

PLAYING OTHER SPORTS
We must remember, though, that football is not the only professional sport in Britain. The Rich List quoted above contained high earners from motor racing, golf, tennis, rugby and even a Brit earning high wages in the States

through basketball. Wealthy sportspeople can also be found in athletics, boxing, snooker, darts and horse racing.

In recent years many of the more traditionally amateur sports have become 'open', resulting in more professional playing opportunities than ever before. Some of these sports are detailed below.

Rugby Union

Rugby has been a professional sport for a number of years now, and the players have now organised a 'union', The Professional Rugby Players' Association, to look after their interests. Like soccer, rugby clubs in Britain are now swamped with foreign players, making less opportunities for British players to earn a living here. There are more than 500 full-time professionals at top level rugby clubs and fewer than this in the lower division clubs which obviously cannot afford to pay high wages or maintain big squads. Wages also vary according to the prestige of the club, with top players earning over £100k p.a. and lower paid professionals approximately £15,000 p.a.

Like soccer, British players are still in big demand abroad, and even players of lesser ability can still find clubs to play for in the developing rugby nations, although whether a living wage would be available here is debatable. Many foreign clubs offer 'packages' which generally means assistance with finding employment and a place to live, sometimes travel expenses and/or a small playing fee might be included. It all really depends on how big a club you are joining, and how good a player you are.

Finding opportunities

Rugby World was always the magazine to find adverts for 'players wanted'. It is still useful in this respect, but now several websites are springing up on the internet that also offer further opportunities to aspiring professionals. Rugbyrecruit.com and rugbyrugby.com are just two of these. The latter, for example, recently contained these two adverts:

> Need two props, immediate start for
> Tooheys New Cup in Sydney, starting this
> weekend running for 12 weeks.
> Good packages on offer but need immediately.

> Want to play in Australia?
> Must be available from late May to early June.
> Level of play (1–10): 8 & Up job required:
> good packages on offer.

The traffic, however, goes both ways, as recently Reading RFC was asking its members if they could find employment for two young Australians who wanted to play in Britain.

Athletics

Few athletes make a living out of their sport. Even at British League level the majority competing in the first division receive little more than hotel and travel expenses for their efforts. Some receive a little extra through grants and personal sponsorship, but this is rarely enough to live on. It is only the really talented few who make it onto the

Grand Prix circuit and can afford to live comfortably. They then get appearance money, prize money if they are good enough and possibly television royalties.

Generally, money isn't available to pay other athletes. The sport doesn't attract enough paying spectators or television coverage to generate enough income, even from international matches.

It is estimated, however, that more than 300 athletes do make enough money out of their sport to live on. Most of this money comes from being a household name such as Colin Jackson and Steve Cram, and is boosted by regular TV appearances, radio and newspaper interviews, after dinner speeches and personal sponsorship. Linford Christie and Daley Thompson reputedly made more than £1 million in this fashion, so current personalities should expect to accumulate more than this.

For the less fortunate National Lottery funding is still given to those who are considered medal prospects at the major championships or to those developing athletes who are considered future prospects.

A precarious living
Although all of the above sounds very promising, to put it in perspective 300 athletes out of literally thousands who join local athletics clubs is not a great proportion. Plus, don't forget, the opportunities to earn only stretch over approximately four months of the outdoor season and a very short indoor season. Athletes then have to fund more than six months of out of season training. An athlete also reduces their earning potential if they are injured, and if

the injury is major or for a long duration could also lose their sponsorship, training grant and also miss out on prize money and advertising. Very precarious!

TURNING PROFESSIONAL

You have to be really outstanding at your sport if you are to earn money from it. Many sports don't have a wage structure as such, because the competitors make their money by tournament earnings, appearance money and exhibition matches. In these cases it is even more vital to be better than the next person because inferior performances mean an inferior standard of living.

Attendance at the next tournament often incurs travel expenses and hotel bills, so it is probably no surprise to learn that the majority of professionals either scrape a meagre existence from their sport, or are forced into part-time employment, fitting their training and competitions around this. Some are forced to play as an amateur in order to obtain a regular wage, often from non-sports related employment. Ironically, some amateurs make more money through their sport than they would do as a lower level professional.

Being a semi-pro

Unfortunately most sports careers are short, the average being between seven and ten years of full-time employment, depending on the type of sport you play. Contact sports are often at the lower end of career span. As a result most professional clubs encourage their players to improve their qualifications and experience in order to gain employment when their playing career ends. The semi-pro often has an advantage over their full-time counterpart in this respect, because they already have experience of other work and possibly another career to fall back on.

EARNING THROUGH COMPETING

Details of sports from which you can make enough money to live on would fill a book like this. Listed below are just some of them. If your sport is not included here it does not mean that it is not possible to make a living from it, but the best way to find out if this is possible is to contact your national organising body. The more popular of these are listed in Chapter 5.

If you would like more specific information about these sports look in the appropriate publications in the book information section of Chapter 9.

angling	ice hockey	soccer
athletics	judo	speedway
badminton	karting	squash
basketball	motor racing	surfing
bmx	mountain biking	swimming
boxing	power boating	table tennis
cricket	rally driving	ten pin bowling
cycling	rugby league	tennis
darts	rugby union	volleyball
equestrianism	skiing	waterskiing
golf	snooker	windsurfing
horse racing		

It is vital to stress again that not all (or even many) of the sports on this list are wage-earning. Most depend on players performing well in tournaments and accumulating prize money, or receiving appearance money. Of course this can also be boosted by advertising, sponsorship, television appearance and exhibition fees.

Sponsorship

Sports like canoeing, where professionals survive merely on sponsorship, that they themselves or their association raise, are not included in the list. It would be unfair to include these as the world of sponsorship is extremely fickle. Companies often withdraw sponsorship when there is a downturn in the economic climate, leaving many recipients high and dry.

Sponsorship is, however, the backbone of British sport. Most sports rely on it, to varying degrees, to provide an existence for their professional competitors that would otherwise be impossible. There can be no doubt that without sponsorship there would be far fewer professional sportspeople.

A number of professionals also supplement their earnings by giving demonstrations and holding coaching clinics, snooker is a good example of this, but if you compete regularly you have limited time to give to such work.

Going abroad

There are also several sports in which competitors find it difficult to earn a living in Britain, but by moving abroad may be able to do so. Cycling, powerboating, judo, skateboarding, snowboarding, swimming, squash, surfing and windsurfing are amongst these. Volleyball is typical of them all; we have several British players competing in clubs in Belgium, France and Switzerland because they can't make enough money out of their sport in their own country.

Golf pros

Being a professional takes on another meaning, however, in golf more than in other sports. Here, if you make money through playing you are called a tournament professional, whereas if you make your living through instructing, organising tournaments and running the golf shop, you would be called a club pro. If you are interested in becoming either of these you need to contact the PGA whose details are in Chapter 5.

WOMEN IN SPORT

In the previous edition of this book it was reported that there were fewer females than males in professional sport . Whilst this is still true, things are improving. Last year the Women's Sport Foundation reported that 589 females received elite athlete lottery funding, which was 48 per cent of the overall total, even though on average women make up only around 17 per cent of the membership of sporting organisations.

Prize money

Prize money in women's sport also continues to improve from that quoted in the previous edition. Last year the men's singles winner at Wimbledon received £655,000 and the women's, although still less, narrowed the gap by gaining £625,000. Conversely though, the winner of the Men's British Open at golf earned in excess of £720,000, whereas the winner of the Women's British Open received only £160,000.

Wages

So there is still some room for improvement as regards prize money for the ladies, but what about the opportunites for wage earning in general?

Last year there were also approximately 106,000 women in Britain compared with 155,000 men in full-time employment in sports related jobs, eg recreation, culture and sport. They earned on average £19,000 compared with £23,000 for men. So, again, there is room for improvement.

Some women's sports, like football, despite greatly improving their profile, lag way behind the men with regards to earnings. Despite making the World Cup quarter finals most of the women in the team fail to make a living out of the sport with the majority being students or having a full-time job. Their clubs cannot afford to pay them. However they do get paid £400 a session for national squad training and matches, with an extra £100 for personal appearances. Faye White probably has the highest profile of all the players as she is both Arsenal and England Captain. She works as a sport development officer to earn a living. In contrast Arsenal men's captain, Thierry Henry, has just signed a new contract which allegedly now earns him £130k a week!

LIVING ON PRIZE MONEY

Relying on prize money is a very risky way of making a living. The number of tournaments giving huge amounts of prize money are minimal, and the bigger the pot the more sportsmen, from all around the world, who will be chasing it. So your chances of success are minimal. Add to this the chance that at the time of this major tournament you may be injured, ill or off form, and you can see how risky it can be to rely on this way of financially supporting yourself, let alone a family. That said, tournaments often provide prize money for lower placed finishers as well as the winners, enabling 'professionals' to eke out a living merely by being 'placed' in competitions throughout the season.

What's available

Two good examples of the range of prize money available at major tournaments this year could be illustrated by the All England Tennis Championships, which is better known internationally simply as 'Wimbledon', and The Open golf championships.

The total prize money given out at Wimbledon was £10,378,710, split into:

◆ men's events: £5,197,440;
◆ women's events £4,446,490;
◆ mixed doubles £323,120;
◆ invitation events £411,660.

The winner of the men's singles received £655,000, with the runner-up gaining £327,500. Semi-finalists received £163,750 and quarter-finalists £85,150. Fourth-round qualifiers took home £45,850, whilst third round £26,520, second round £16,050 and first-round qualifiers received £9,830.

In the men's doubles the winners received £220,690, with take home earnings for first-round qualifiers of £5,000.

The women's singles winner received £625,000, and first-round qualifiers £7,860. Women's doubles winners received £205,280 and first-round qualifiers £3,960. Finally, mixed doubles winners received £90,000 with first-round qualifiers getting £1,180.

The Open Golf Championships in 2006 were reported to be putting up prize money in excess of the £4 million that had been the given out at the last championship. The first prize was in excess of the £720,000 that was received at Royal Troon.

The prize money at the Weetabix Women's British Open Golf was much lower at £1.05 million, with the champion receiving £160,000, second place £100,000, third place £70,000, down to 65th place still earning £1,550.

TAKING THE PLUNGE

If, despite the drawbacks stated above, you are still determined to make a career out of playing your sport, it would be prudent to:

a) know your market;
b) know your own ability;
c) not aim too high;
d) thoroughly research the opportunities.

Knowing your own ability

Competitors generally assess their ability in the context of the team they are currently playing with, or in the case of individual sports the standard of tournament – local, county, national – that they are able to enter. Obviously, if you are only playing Sunday League football, or club tournament golf, there is little chance that any Football League clubs would be interested in you, or that you would make it through the qualifying tournaments for the British Open. However, strange things can happen, even the best selectors can get it wrong and your situation could be one of them.

When I was the County Schools Coach for under-19 basketball, I advised one of my better players to concentrate on his basketball, at which he had undoubted prospects. Unfortunately he preferred football and he was spending a lot of valuable training and basketball playing time pursuing his football dreams, even though he was only in his sixth form college's second team. He totally ignored my advice and went on to play for Middlesbrough FC and Manchester United. That student, Gary Pallister, also went on to play for England, and now since retirement still earns money as a television pundit.

Being realistic

Occasionally, because of other influences, some prospective professional players can't gauge their ability through conventional methods because they have been out of the sport for a period of time. This could be due to injury, marriage, starting a family, work restrictions, or a multitude of other reasons. The first step in rehabilitation from any of these is primarily to get match fit, and then to approach a local club in order to test out their skills against various standards of competitor.

The golden rule is not to aim too high initially. Start at the bottom and work your way up. During this progression you will be gaining in fitness and improving your playing ability but also, just as importantly, you'll be acquiring knowledge initially of the local scene, then as you improve, the county and hopefully, later the national one.

Researching
Before embarking on any venture it is always wise to find out as much as possible about the market that interests you. Acquire a copy of your sport's specialist magazine, most large libraries carry the most popular of these, and also research it on the internet. Contact the magazines that interest you, and ask if they have printed any articles covering professionalism and opportunities in your sport. They will generally have back copies for sale so will be pleased to furnish you with this information in order to make a sale.

The next step would then be to contact any clubs or associations mentioned in these articles that you think will be of assistance. Other useful sources of information can be local and national newspapers and local sports centres. Chapter 4 deals with this in greater detail.

If you are already playing at a high level you will probably already know someone who makes a living out of their sport and who knows what the terms of employment and 'work' conditions are like. If you don't know someone, ask around. Somebody in your club will no doubt have a contact who could help you.

Making your own opportunities
If, surprisingly, through your enquiries you don't uncover any opportunities, then try to make some for yourself. Place an advert on your club's noticeboard, in the local

newsagents or at your sports centre. If these cheaper alternatives don't bear fruit you might consider splashing out on advertising in your sport's national magazine or on the internet. Let players and officials of your club, or rival clubs, know that you are looking for employment. You never know what may turn up. Once you have exhausted these avenues try writing to the national governing body of your sport. You can find the addresses of these organisations in Chapter 5.

CASE STUDY

The best time of Ian's life

Ian found playing much more attractive than coaching football.

He was one of the lucky few who went straight into a career as a pro footballer immediately after leaving school. His playing career began with Hartlepool United before transferring to Fulham. Later he joined Oxford United, but unfortunately an injury to his knee cut short his career, which nevertheless extended to more than ten years. Quite a good duration for a contact sport.

Nowadays Ian works at one of the local colleges as a football coach. He enjoys his job there, but obviously finds it very different from his playing career, which he describes as 'the best time of his life.'

Life in soccer was not only more glamorous and fun, but also the salary was a lot higher than he currently receives. Adapting to all of these changes was a real culture shock for him.

If he could make any changes, Ian would have completed all of his coaching awards whilst still playing. This would have enabled him to take up the many offers he received to stay in professional sport.

Ian also advises any youngsters thinking of pursing this option to go for it 100 per cent, *but* don't forget that at some time it is going to end, so look after the money!

Ian gained the first FA coaching badge before retiring from soccer and is now nearing completing his final one. After this he is considering possibly changing tack and qualifying as a teacher.

TAKING THE PLUNGE – CHECKLIST

◆ Know your market – do you thoroughly understand the complexities of the sport that you are hoping to work in?

◆ Know your ability – are you good enough to make the grade? Dreams alone won't do it.

◆ Don't aim too high, too soon – take your time and use that time constructively.

◆ Research – magazines, guides, brochures, newspapers, internet, etc.

◆ Enquire – through teammates, opponents, coaches, administrators, etc.

- Advertise – on noticeboards, sports magazines, newspapers, the internet, etc.

- Contact – local and national organisers.

COACHING AND INSTRUCTING

You can gain valuable experience coaching and instructing sportspeople without holding a recognised qualification, but this is not recommended. First of all it will be almost impossible to gain paid employment without one, but more importantly you will not be covered if somebody injures themselves (participants and spectators) in one of your sessions. If you hold a recognised coaching award it is almost 100 per cent certain that they will provide you with insurance cover for free, or in some cases at very low cost.

To achieve the basic level coaching award is very easy in most sports, and this is dealt with in more detail in Chapter 6. A list of organisers of these awards is contained in Chapter 5.

Where is the demand?

The demand for coaches varies both in the UK and abroad, but as a general rule there are always opportunities for employment in:

- sports centres and swimming baths;
- private sports clubs (soccer, tennis, squash, fitness, etc);
- outdoor pursuits centres;
- local authorities (sports development officer, management, etc);

◆ commercial organisations (ski companies, activity holiday companies, etc).

CASE STUDY

Gareth loves his job as a golf pro

Gareth's mother and father were both keen golfers and took him for his first game when he was about 7 years old. From then on he was hooked.

Gareth was good at a multitude of other sports including cricket, skiing and soccer and even started a sports science degree at university, but it was golf that was his first love. He was playing county golf and had won numerous tournaments when he decided to try his luck on the Euro Pro Tour. Unfortunately this didn't work out as he was earning barely enough money to live on, so he pursued the next option working as a club pro.

He took the PGA National Diploma, which involves everything from teaching to sports science and club repair, and is an absolute requirement for this work.

After qualifying Gareth became one of the Club Professionals at Wynyard Golf Club where he loves his job. He easily makes enough money to live on, but this fluctuates with the season. He is paid only a small basic wage for running the pro shop, but gets a commission on sales. He is also really pleased that at this club he keeps all fees for teaching, whereas at other clubs the head pro normally takes a big percentage of these.

So Gareth is really happy with his career, as not only does it provide him with a good living wage, but also gives him the opportunity to play as much golf as he wants. He also loves many other aspects of the game: the fact that you never stop learning, the social side of it, travelling around Britain and Europe to other courses, seeing people who he has coached, especially kids, develop and meeting so many interesting people.

Gareth would advise anybody considering golf as a career to first of all be realistic, and consider if they are good enough. He has seen so many fail because they thought they were better than they actually were.

Then they should decide early which direction they are going to take. Try for a golf scholarship, if they have the ability. If they are going to try out as a tournament pro they should go at it 100 per cent as they can always take their PGA awards at a later date, and the experience that they have gained will always be useful.

WORKING IN SPORTS-RELATED EMPLOYMENT

There are numerous jobs connected with sport which, although you might not be taking part directly in your own sport, may prove satisfying merely by being associated with it. For example:

◆ community recreation officer;
◆ county development officer;
◆ groundsman;
◆ manager of a leisure facility;

- sports manufacturers rep;
- outdoor activities instructor;
- P.E. teacher;
- physiotherapist;
- retail manager/assistant;
- sports centre assistant;
- sports journalist;
- sports photographer.

CASE STUDY

Working at a leisure facility

Jim had worked at numerous jobs including in the NHS, the NAAFI and Qantas, before gaining employment in the leisure sector. Conversely, Ian had taken employment in leisure straight after leaving school, initially working in swimming pools and sports centres. They now both form part of the management team at a large leisure facility/athletics stadium.

Jim's official title is Principal Leisure Manager, and Ian is Recreation Officer. They both agree that they prefer their present jobs to anything they have done previously, but for different reasons.

Ian originally intended joining the army, but is glad he didn't as he now gets a lot of pleasure working with the public.

Jim prefers this job because of the variety. The hours are long, but the rewards are there. He wanted to point out that the job also has its downsides, like dealing with irate customers and slow bureaucracy. Nevertheless, he still enjoys it.

Ian advises anybody considering this as a career to look in the weekly ILAM bulletins (see Glossary) or local newspapers for situations vacant. You don't need any qualifications to begin with, but a certificate in first aid would give you a head start. Once employed you would be trained on the job, and expected to take courses such as safe electricity at work, and handling aggression and violence.

TEACHING

Many schoolchildren are inspired to a career in sport by their own P.E. teacher. They probably get the impression that the P.E. teacher's job entails running around playing sport all day with the pupils. In fact nothing could be further from the truth. The P.E. teacher's workload generally consists of the following.

- Being a form teacher; registering their class and taking them to assembly every morning.

- Dealing with any classwork, homework, discipline and truancy problems.

- Taking lessons in sport, but probably also the second teaching subject that they trained in.

- Collecting in valuables, dealing with lost kit and suspiciously examining sick notes.

- Filling in assessment forms for every pupil in every class.

◆ Writing reports for all of their pupils.

◆ Giving up lunchtimes, evenings and weekends, without extra pay, to run school teams.

◆ Attending staff meetings, as well as those for faculties, departments and houses.

◆ Attending parents' evenings.

◆ Lesson preparation and marking coursework.

◆ Telephoning parents and other schools for fixtures.

◆ Administering first aid.

◆ Ordering new equipment and maintaining the old.

You can see that a lot of the P.E. teacher's workload is taken up by doing work that is not directly connected to sport. The most enjoyable part is taking the children for lessons, but this only accounts for a fraction of the time, and remember this is *teaching* not actually participating in sport. In fact a directive sent out by the Department of Education several years ago stated quite categorically that teachers should not join in any contact sports with the children. Contact sports included soccer, basketball and hockey amongst others.

So the opportunities for P.E. teachers to play sports and maintain their level of skill and fitness, within lesson times, is very limited. Nevertheless, P.E. teaching is a very satisfying and rewarding job.

Qualifications

In order to teach you need to have acquired the

appropriate teaching qualification at university. This is normally a Bachelor of Education degree, or a PGCE for graduates already possessing a degree. Before being accepted at university applicants will need to have passed at least two A levels. P.E. teachers will also be expected to have achieved a high level of proficiency in at least one sport.

CASE STUDY

Steve has to choose between teaching and football as a career

Steve was always going to be a footballer – his father played in the Northern League and his uncle had been a pro with Colchester. The only decision he had to make was whether he was going to be able to make a career out of it.

He had been on the books at both Middlesbrough and Sunderland and could probably have earned a living playing in the Unibond League, but he decided to make a career out of teaching and playing football mainly for enjoyment. So now he plays as a semi-pro and captain of Billingham Town in the Northern League.

Steve thoroughly enjoys his job as a teacher, but if he could have made any changes says that he would probably have taken up teaching at a later age, having first taken his soccer coaching to a higher level and possibly worked abroad. He would have still taken the same Sports Science degree at Carnegie, Leeds, as that gives more choice of career at the end of the course, but he is certain he would have eventually become a teacher all the same.

THE ARMED FORCES

One of the Army's past adverts read:

> Who encourages you to play sport during working hours? *The Army does.*

This confirms one of the great attractions of a services career to sportspeople. The higher level that you play your sport at, the more time you'll get off to pursue it. In other words you are being paid to play sport.

Unfortunately, it's not quite as simple as that and there are other demands and responsibilities that come with a services career. Amongst others you could be asked to serve in a war zone.

Also:

◆ You have to be able to cope with living in a barracks with other recruits.

◆ You have to be able to cope with discipline.

◆ You normally have to complete basic training before you qualify for time off to play any sport.

If you join the Navy remember that competing in your sport is very difficult if you are on board a ship. The Army and the RAF are therefore able to provide greater opportunities for sporting achievement as they offer more land based careers.

Becoming a Physical Training Instructor (PTI) isn't absolutely necessary to pursue your sport. Sometimes it is better to work in another trade, leaving yourself fresh and enthusiastic for participation. It also gives you another avenue of opportunity to pursue when your sports career is over.

CASE STUDY

Playing to the max in the Army

I met Doug at a county rugby match and was immediately interested in his role in the Armed Forces in relation to his participation in sport. His job in the Army was as a mechanic with the Royal Engineers, but he was given time off to partake in his representative sports. He not only played county rugby, but also for his regiment, the Army and the Combined Services. For each of these he was given leave to train and play. He was currently only working for two and a half days per week, but told me that he had just made the regiment's basketball team and so expected to spend even less time on base.

I was seriously considering joining up myself!

TAKING A YEAR (OR MORE) OUT

The vast majority of students who decide to take a year out generally want to see the world and earn money at the same time. Chapter 3 looks at the different options abroad. However, some students prefer to stay in Britain for this study break. The reasons for doing so vary, but some of the main ones are as follows:

1. They want to gain experience in industry before embarking on university or college.
2. They simply want a short break from the educational system before returning to working and studying for exams.
3. They want to pursue their sport to a higher level without the burden of exams or a career.
4. They want to earn some money before becoming a penniless student at university.

CASE STUDY

Steve decides that studying could get in the way

After leaving school Steve had arranged a year's work experience in industry through the Year in Industry scheme run by Durham University. After this he intended to study at Sheffield University for a degree in electrical engineering and electronics. He had decided on this course of action because:

◆ He wanted a break from the pressures of theory work and exams.
◆ It would help him in future job applications to have this experience behind him.
◆ He wanted to earn some money before becoming an impoverished student.
◆ He wanted to train for athletics.

Steve had one last chance to become an international athlete at Junior Men's level. It would be much harder the following year when he moves up into the Senior ranks. He had been highly placed in the National Decathlon rankings the previous year when he was a year younger than most of the athletes above him. This season was his last chance; now it was all or nothing.

When interviewed Steve reflected on his decision. He thought that he had made the right decision to take a year out to train for athletics, but, if he had the time over again, he would not have taken the same job. He would have worked part-time as putting so much effort into his work often left him too tired to train properly. Otherwise he had no regrets.

Unfortunately, Steve didn't gain his international vest as a serious injury whilst pole vaulting cut short his season. After qualifying Steve also decided that engineering was not for him, and now earns a fortune as a mortgage advisor.

STUDYING WHILST COACHING AND COMPETING

Gaining a place at college or university is an ideal way of participating in and improving your sport. The added bonus is that you come out at the end of your course with a qualification that many employers find desirable.

Sports scholarships started, and are still nowadays predominantly available, in the USA. However other countries, including Britain, are quickly catching up with their system.

Since the last edition of this book there have been significant changes in the funding of our better sports-people who choose to pursue a course of higher education whilst competing. It is still, however, nowhere near as financially rewarding as it is in the USA and there is still no structured national directive on this. It is also left to individual universities and colleges to decide whether or not they want to offer scholarships and/or bursaries to talented sportspeople.

For example, Durham University has chosen not to offer scholarships to students starting university, but does offer them to students who have already gained one degree (postgraduates) and are continuing in higher education, whereas Edinburgh University offers sports bursaries of up to £1,500 per annum, but mainly for golf. The leader in the field seems to be Birmingham which offers scholarships in golf of up to of £10,000 a year and other sports of up to £5,000.

The TASS scheme

This improvement was made possible, on the whole, by a major advancement in funding organised by the Government and Sports Councils, called the Talented Athlete Scholarship Scheme, or TASS as it is better known. The word 'Athlete' in the title is used in its broadest sense, unfortunately imported from America, to mean sportsmen and sportswomen.

The TASS scheme supports 47 sports in total, ranging from archery to waterskiing, 15 of these are disability sports.

To quote their website:

The programme awards Scholarships and Bursaries to talented sports people that are committed to combining their sport and education. It aims to reduce the drop out of talented athletes from sport and supports and develops the talent of today for sporting success in the future.

Detailed below is a list of sports scholarships and bursaries which were recently offered in the UK. To gain one an applicant is expected to be at or near international level. Again, to quote the TASS website:

TASS aims to bridge the gap between non-funding grass roots sport and world-class sport. Therefore it is the responsibility of sporting National Governing Bodies (NGBs) to identify their TASS athletes. This procedure is done in conjunction with higher educational institutes (HEIs) who are also given the opportunity to nominate athletes.

Individual athletes may be nominated by other agencies but the NGB must approve the application. If you feel that you would meet your sport's eligibility criteria please contact your NGB for further information. The NGBs have the final decision on TASS athlete selection.

There are two types of TASS awards, Bursaries and Scholarships. For more information please see Bursary information and Scholarship information.

To be eligible athletes must hold a valid Great Britain passport and be eligible to compete in their sport for GB. Athletes must also reside at an English address or be studying at an English HEI. Current world-class funded athletes (Start, Potential and Performance) cannot receive additional funding from TASS.

More extensive information on national scholarships and bursaries can be sourced through your local library or on the internet.

Scholarships that have recently been available

Examples of what has been on offer recently are given below, however please bear in mind that this is by no means a complete list and that details may have changed since going to press.

- ◆ Aberdeen University – more than ten sports bursaries given each year. Normally £1,000.

- ◆ University of Birmingham – scholarships in a range of sports up to £10,000.

- ◆ University of Bristol – 12 Vice-Chancellor's scholarships available annually at £3,000.

- ◆ Brunel University – scholarships in a multitude of sports up to £3,000 p.a.

- ◆ University of Cambridge – website contains details of a multitude of scholarships that are too numerous to list (see Chapter 5).

- ◆ Cardiff University – bursaries in a range of sports up to £750 p.a.

- Coventry University – scholarships in a multitude of sports up to £2,000 p.a.

- De Montfort University – 25 scholarships are available of up to £1,000 p.a.

- Durham University – scholarships only available for postgraduate courses.

- Edinburgh University – golf and other sports bursaries up to £1,500 p.a.

- Exeter University – ten scholarships of £5,000 p.a. for a variety of subjects including sport.

- Glasgow University – up to £1,000 p.a. over a range of sports.

- Heriot-Watt University – golf and other sports scholarships up to £1,500 p.a.

- Leeds Metropolitan University – up to £3,000 p.a. in athletics, cricket, golf, tennis and possibly other sports.

- Loughborough University – up to £1,000 p.a. for students of at least Junior International level.

- University of Manchester – sport scholarships of up to £2,000.

- Newcastle University – more than 30 TAS Scholarships and other bursaries.

- University of Northumbria – small sports scholarships available.

- Oxford University – numerous scholarships, but only given to students of outstanding academic ability – see website (details in Chapter 5).

- Queen's University Belfast – bursaries up to £4,300 available.

- St Andrew's University – information on website regarding golf scholarships.

- Stirling University – scholarships for national level competitors.

- University of Strathclyde – golf and other sports up to £1,000 p.a.

- University of Sunderland – sports scholarships of £1,500.

- University of Surrey – normally offering scholarships up to £3,000, and bursaries of up to £1,000 to talented young people.

- Swansea University – scholarship of £1,000 p.a. renewable for three years.

- University of Teesside – offers sports bursaries of up to £2,000.

- University of Ulster – 20 scholarships up to £1,000 for world-class performers.

- University of Wales Aberystwyth – scholarships up to £2,000 p.a.

- University of Wales Bangor – five scholarships of £500 minimum.

- University of Wales Newport – sports scholarships and bursaries available.

- University of Worcester – good scholarships for cricket and also basketball.

CASE STUDY

Kevin helped to pay his way through university by coaching tennis

Kevin had always been a good tennis player and after leaving Millfield School decided to continue his sport through university. He studied at Bedford and supplemented his student grant by coaching at the local Riverside Club. Fortunately Kevin already held his LTA Club Performance Coaching Award, so picking up a coaching job was relatively easy. Even when he later qualified and moved into teaching Kevin coached at numerous different clubs. He could have made tennis coaching his full time profession but decided, despite the fact that it is much harder and more demanding, to make teaching his vocation. He chose this route because teaching gives him more variety and ultimately more enjoyment, as well as being a regular, more dependable wage with a good pension at the end.

When asked if there was anything he would change if he had the chance, he replied that he wouldn't change a thing, except maybe when he was of school age he would have spent more time playing tennis.

Just prior to this book being published Kevin was still thoroughly enjoying his job, having just taken one of his teams to the England finals at *rugby*!

COACHING OPPORTUNITIES WITHIN COLLEGES

The American trend of offering 'graduate assistantships' to coaches wanting to further their education has, to a minor degree, been adopted in Britain. Manchester and the University of Bath have, along with a handful of other universities, offered these in the past. Unfortunately, it is still not as commonplace as in the States.

If you would like to pursue this option then either enquire about availability at your chosen university or contact the British Universities Sports Association at 20–24 Kings Bench Street, London SE1 0QX tel: 020 7633 5080 website: busa.org.uk.

WORKING IN CLOSE PROXIMITY TO YOUR SPORT

Working in a job that keeps you close to your sport, without actually participating, can be a good idea as it maintains your interest and freshness. There are countless opportunities, too numerous to mention, in every type of employment. So if you are interested in this option you need to first choose the region where you would be involved in sport, then the area in which you can obtain accommodation and then try to gain employment some- where between the two.

Your first task must be to contact the Jobcentre in that area to find out the range of jobs that are available. If nothing appeals to you then you could try contacting the sports club that you are intending joining, and even opposing clubs who might be interested in 'stealing' your services by offering a lucrative job. If they suggest that you visit them you could use this as an opportunity to check out:

- noticeboards at the local sports centres;
- noticeboards at youth hostels;
- situations vacant in the local newspapers;
- specialist newspapers and magazines connected to your sport.

You could also take the opportunity to place your own advert when visiting these places, plus other places such as supermarkets and shops, offering your services.

VOLUNTARY WORK

Although many people considering voluntary work are interested in working abroad, it is also possible to pursue this course in Britain. Hospitals and care centres rely on this type of help, and organisations such as Help the Aged and Oxfam often have vacancies for volunteers, many of these offering expenses.

You will find this option is covered more extensively in Chapter 3. Although it deals with working abroad, much of the advice is also relevant to Britain. The suggested reading is particularly important if you are considering this as a way forward.

SELF-ASSESSMENT EXERCISE

1. Have you decided that it is definitely Britain that you want to work in?

2. Which option of utilising your sport most appeals to you?

3. Do you have the required level of skill and qualifications to enable you to follow this path?

4. Do you know who to contact to pursue your chosen sport?

3

Examining the Different Options Abroad

Working abroad is sometimes the preferred option of many sportspeople as not only does it give them the opportunity to enjoy paid employment in their favourite sport, but also they gain experience in coaching or playing in a different environment. Further benefits are also gaining useful references, which can be utilised when seeking employment back at home, while at the same time experiencing different cultures.

PLAYING AWAY

Becoming wealthy through your sport abroad is not easy. David Beckham and Michael Olowokandi are the exceptions rather than the rule. You need to be absolutely outstanding to be a top earner whatever your sport! You don't, however, need to be *that* good if your aim is just to use your sport as an opportunity to travel, or earn a moderate living whilst experiencing a different environment.

Choosing the right country

If your chosen sport is soccer and you want to play abroad then don't expect to be snapped up by teams in Europe or South America – they *will* expect you to be brilliant! But if you tried a club in Asia, Africa, or North America your chances would be much better.

Alternatively, if your sport is rugby, which few countries in the world play better than Britain, then approaching clubs in Europe or the Americas could be advantageous.

The best course of action is always to be realistic in your aims and to follow the procedure we introduced in Chapter 2:

◆ know your market;
◆ know your own ability;
◆ research;
◆ don't aim too high.

CASE STUDY

Stu swaps Stockton for Michigan
Stu had hit a crossroads in his life. His current job was only OK, but his rugby career was on the slide. He also felt that he had not done enough or seen enough of the world. He was quite a typical case.

He had left school to go straight to university and then, once qualified, back to school again; this time teaching.

So he decided to call in an offer that he had received whilst at college, and at the end of the summer holidays boarded a plane for Detroit.

Stu played rugby for Michigan RFC whilst staying with the club vice captain and looking for employment. A condition of his visa was that he had a return ticket home, but he hoped that he would have picked up a job before the expiry date and not have to use it. Unfortunately, the rugby club was based in the university town of Ann Arbor, and all of the part-time or low-paid jobs were taken up by students. Maybe he should have researched this a little more.

So, although enjoying his rugby enormously, he returned home happy with his experience, but jobless. He had been offered one job coaching at a sports centre, but that was to start two months in the future and with money rapidly running out he decided to use his return ticket.

Once home another really good job offer arrived, but Stu had now happily settled back into teaching at a really good school.

If only . . .

Knowing the market

Maybe if Stu had asked a few more questions before going abroad he would have realised that although his ability as a county player would give him numerous opportunities to play in the States, the possibilities of picking up employment were limited.

The USA does not have the professional set-up in rugby that we have in Europe so earning money purely through playing was not going to happen. Being paid to coach might have been a possibility, but that would have had to be with a bigger club or college. Picking up a job outside of sport might have been more realistic in another town: even more likely in another country.

Knowing your ability

This is generally quite easy. If you are playing in the national league of your sport there is a good chance that your level of performance would be welcomed in most clubs around the world.

Things take on a different perspective, though, if you can't even make the starting line-up of your *local* league team. The chances are that most countries would have numerous players of your ability, so consequently your market would be very restricted.

As already mentioned in Chapter 2, even the best team selectors make mistakes and your failure to make the team could be one of these. If you are confident this has happened, and you believe you are a better player than your playing record suggests, you are still advised to exercise some caution. Don't go to all the expense and upheaval of travelling abroad on what could become a fruitless and frustrating mission. Test yourself out in Britain by changing clubs. If you achieve more success there, then you know that your previous selectors were wrong.

The 'open' revolution

In recent years many sports have gone 'open'. In other words, sports that were ostensibly amateur now allow their players to earn money from competing.

Two prime examples of these are Rugby Union and athletics. The opportunities in these sports for the paid employment of quality players and coaches are steadily on the increase. Advertisements for these, and many other newly professionalised sports, regularly appear in their own specialist magazines.

This is all very well for sports that advertise openly for players, but not all sports do. How, then, do you find the opportunities in sports that recruit from within their own system?

GETTING CONTACTS ABROAD

Researching
Research is absolutely vital! This was covered in Chapter 2, and the same methods for seeking opportunities in the UK can be used abroad.

When you contact a magazine ask them if they published an article covering sport in the country of your choice. Even if clubs in these countries haven't committed money to advertising for players, they are probably still on the lookout for good talent. Write to any clubs or associations mentioned in these articles.

Sometimes tourist brochures and pocket guidebooks about your chosen country contain a section on sport. Use the same approach with these too.

Another source of useful information is newspapers, in particular the weekend editions of these. Saturday and Sunday editions, but also sometimes midweek versions, often contain comprehensive travel sections. Travel and holiday companies sometimes contain, often brief, sections on sport in certain countries.

Once again, the internet carries a wealth of information on opportunities abroad, with employment and sport being just two of the categories on offer.

Chapter 4 deals with accessing the internet in more detail.

Finding the openings

Using the internet is now a great way of discovering the opportunities that exist in a sport (see Chapter 4), but some sports still prefer to target their employees through specialist magazines. A recent copy of *Horse and Hound* contained no fewer than 29 adverts offering employment. The jobs advertised included college lecturer, sales rep, farrier, riders and numerous grooms. Two of the opportunities were for overseas work. Chapter 9 gives contact information for many of the prominent specialist magazines.

The internet, however, contained hundreds of opportunities to work abroad including fitness instructors in Bermuda, basketball instructors in Canada, canoeing instructors in Egypt, cycling leaders in Greece, golf instructors in Lanzarote and soccer coaches in the USA, amongst a multitude of others.

Making enquiries

If you are lucky you will know someone who has previously been to a country of interest to you and knows what the playing conditions are like. If you don't, then ask around. Somebody in your club may know a friend of a friend who can help. Finally, if your lines of enquiry dry up, put an advert on your club noticeboard, and that of any other clubs that you visit. Sportspeople are really friendly people. You will probably be amazed how much assistance you receive – even from players you considered were deadly rivals.

Using local expertise

If you are considering playing abroad you must already be playing at a reasonable level. As a result you should have some contact with your local and national coaches, or at least know their contact information. Use them. Ask them if they know of any opportunities to play abroad. They, in their years of playing and coaching, have probably made numerous contacts who might be willing to assist you in joining a foreign club.

The direct method is usually the most productive approach, but there are others.

Advertising yourself

If throughout your enquiries you can't find any openings or opportunities, try to create some for yourself.

Place an advertisement in your sport's magazine, or on the internet (see Figure 3). If you are keen to go to a particular region then contact the tourist information office for that area and enquire about advertising there. They may be able to sort out some free advertising for you, or at worst give you the addresses, and other information on their free papers and daily and evening newspapers. If you can write the advertisement in the native language this is likely to get a more positive reaction. If you can't do this you may be able to get assistance from the tourist office, one of your old school's language teachers, or a friend who speaks the language.

British county-level Basketball Player, 19 years old, 1.94m tall, fluent in Spanish, is looking to compete for a club in Spain during the coming season.

Assistance with accommodation and employment would be appreciated. If you can help please telephone 01234 567890 or write to PO Box 321, Sportown, England

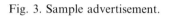

Fig. 3. Sample advertisement.

Advertising in this way was previously tried quite successfully by two South African athletes who contacted *Athletics Weekly*. They quickly became established as members of a prominent club in the south of England.

Contacting National Organisers
Again, as in Chapter 2, write to the national governing body of your sport and ask them if they can put you in touch with the national body of the country you would like to visit.

You can find the addresses of NGBs in Chapter 5.

Approaching the embassy
Another option is to write directly to the embassy of your preferred country, telling them of your intentions. Ask them for the addresses of their national associations and any other contacts they might have. It is unlikely that they would know of any opportunities that exist as they are more politically orientated – but it does no harm to ask.

The majority of embassies are based in London and their addresses can be found by looking through the London telephone directories, or again through searching the internet. Most main libraries can help with this, as they generally have these directories, but if not the librarian will probably know of alternative sources. As a last resort, because this now costs money, you could phone one of the numerous directory enquiry companies.

Trying pot luck
The least desirable option is to travel to the country of choice and seek opportunities whilst you are there.

If you decide to use this method you must plan carefully and make contingency plans for the homeward journey if your finances reach a predetermined critically low level.

This is obviously not the most recommended way of seeking a placement. A lot of the people I know who have tried this return home dejected, but have enjoyed an extended holiday abroad due to trying. Some have stayed, but ended up working in a job not connected to their sport whilst still hoping their dream will materialise. The majority, though, simply return home penniless, but normally quite happy with the experience.

If you do, however, still decide to go ahead with this option, you will have more chance of success if you are organised in the way you approach the task in hand. Focus your efforts.

Focusing your efforts
Once you arrive at your destination, focus your efforts on the locations that are most likely to yield results. Check out:

- noticeboards at sports centres;
- noticeboards at youth hostels;
- Job Centres (or their equivalent);
- the situations vacant section in the local newspaper;
- specialist newspapers like *Overseas Jobs Express*;
- noticeboards at supermarkets.

If all of the above fails then place your own advertisements in these places.

Finally, and probably most enjoyably, find the liveliest bar in town and talk to the locals, if you are competent in their language. Many, many jobs have been arranged over a friendly drink in a bar or at the local golf course or sports centre.

Relying on pot luck is the least recommended course of action as it can be very time consuming, often producing little or no results. It will almost definitely be more expensive than you imagined, and very often depressing.

However, after criticising this method, many people known to myself have used this approach over the years to pick up good jobs ranging from ski resorts in Europe to hotels in the Far East.

CASE STUDY

Two Aussies strike it lucky

Whilst skiing in Les Orres in the French Alps several seasons ago I met two Australian backpackers, Luke and Jon, who came into the hotel and asked the manager if there were any temporary jobs going. Even though they were trying pot luck they had taken an intelligent approach to finding jobs. Firstly they had targeted a highly likely source of employment and secondly they made sure that they carried references with them from their most recent employers. They were working their way around Europe, staying approximately one month at a time in each resort. They started work the very next day: one in the kitchen and the other as a barman.

As expected they didn't stay long. It was rumoured that a month later they were in another hotel in Alp d'Huez.

MAKING CONTACTS ABROAD – CHECKLIST

1. Know your market – choose the right country.

2. Know your ability – are you good enough for sport in this country, or would another country provide an easier market?

3. Don't aim too high – better to work up from the bottom than receive no offers at all.

4. Research – magazines, guides, the internet, brochures, newspapers, etc relevant to your chosen country.

5. Enquire – teammates, opponents, coaches, administrators, etc.

6. Advertise – on the internet, noticeboards, foreign and UK magazines and newspapers.

7. Contact – national organisers and embassies.

8. Pot luck – once there try sports centres, sports clubs, youth hostels, job centres, situations vacant, super-markets and bars.

COACHING AND INSTRUCTING

If you would like to coach abroad then it would be extremely advisable, although not always absolutely necessary, to hold a British coaching award. Many 'beginner' level awards are relatively easy to achieve and also quite inexpensive. Many Level One awards do not even require an exam to be taken at the end of the course, merely full attendance.

You can find out more about coaching awards in Chapter 6.

Why go to the expense of qualifying?

British coaching awards are generally held in high esteem abroad and are an excellent springboard in your quest for employment. They are well worth the investment. They generally also provide insurance cover for yourself, but check on this as they might not cover foreign countries.

A list of organisers of these awards is contained in Chapter 5 and there is more information on them in Chapter 6.

The same approach for gaining employment as a player can be used for coaching/instructing, so you might wish to refer to the earlier section in this chapter. In addition, you should note that many more coaches than players are now being sought through the internet. British coaches, more so than players, are in demand abroad. This is because most countries prefer to import a coach to develop their own talent rather than bring foreign players into their domestic game.

Britain typifies this approach – we often import ice hockey and basketball coaches from North America, but export soccer coaches to them.

Clubs generally work on the concept that if they import a good player he or she is still only one player. They may improve the team immediately, but a coach can develop dozens of players who will enhance their team for the long-term future.

Identifying the demand
As in the first edition good soccer, athletics and rugby coaches are in demand throughout the world, but you need to apply to the less developed countries to gain a coaching appointment in our less successful sports. Many of the posts available are through voluntary organisations which despite the name generally pay a 'wage' (see below).

The leisure industry continues to be the big, booming success story in commerce. There are numerous organisations actively seeking coaches and instructors to look after sportspeople of all ages on their activity holiday courses. Details of these companies are included in Chapter 9.

Activity holiday companies are now not only employing instructors in the traditional slot of our schools' summer holiday period, but increasingly all year round. This is due to the enormous number of family holidays that are now being taken further afield in warmer climates than found in northern Europe. The tropics and southern hemisphere are now well within reach and resorts there have been set up to cater for British and European holidaymakers. Due to this, jobs that were once considered as temporary and seasonal now provide employment all year round.

Finding work in the leisure industry
Full-time employment is often achieved by working with the same company in the northern hemisphere in our summer then after that in the southern hemisphere, or working in the mountains as a ski instructor in the winter, and then the same mountains during the summer leading pony trekking tours, walks or rock climbing.

By far the most common way of coaching and instructing in the leisure industry is to work the summer season on the beach as surfing/windsurf/canoe instructor, for example, and then the winter in the mountains instructing snowboarding, skiing, ice skating, etc.

There are many other permutations like this of sports that are possible to combine. Activity holiday companies are constantly advertising for instructors in:

aerobics	pony trekking	squash
archery	sailing	surfing
basketball	scuba diving	swimming
canoeing	self-defence	table tennis
climbing	skateboarding	tennis
fencing	skiing	volleyball
golf	snorkelling	waterskiing
horse riding	snowboarding	windsurfing
ice skating	soccer	yoga
paragliding		

CASE STUDY

Lucky Rob lands a job as a ski guide

Rob was one of those people who seemed to have all the luck. He didn't have to work too hard for his opportunities. Everything just seemed to effortlessly fall into place.

His parents took him skiing to Scotland when he was only 4 years old. Then he went regularly on his school's skiing holidays and became good enough to race for Cleveland Schools in the English Schools Championships.

A few years later, when he was rock climbing in the Vanoise National Park in France, he made the acquaintance of another climber. As they talked together the topic turned to skiing and Rob mentioned that he would love to work in this industry. Of course, with Rob's inherent luck this guy just happened to have a friend who was looking for some ski guides to work the forthcoming season. He took Rob's phone number and promised to get in touch.

Rob heard nothing for quite some time so as the months passed he decided that was just an empty gesture, made in friendly conversation.

Eight months later the phone rang and Rob was offered an interview in France. He dropped everything and sped off to Meribel where he worked the following season.

He loved the job, loved the mountain environment, loved working with the type of people you meet there. He would have returned again but, needing to support himself for the next eight months, took on the commitment of employment, which ended up being permanent.

Maybe he should have read this book! He would then have discovered how he could have achieved these objectives.

Rob says that he would certainly recommend this work to anybody looking for sports employment. The wage isn't brilliant, but easily enough to provide any extras needed, as it is normal for all food and accommodation to be provided. His main advice, though, is that if you are at school or in higher education, to really stick in at your exams, ideally also become a qualified BASI ski instructor, and then send your CV to as many holiday companies as possible. Don't just send to the big companies, either, the smaller independents can be just as productive, as well as fun and rewarding.

VOLUNTEERING

Most people have a misconception about voluntary work abroad because it suggests that you are working for no pay. Yet in the majority of cases this is not true. Remuneration varies greatly, from those organisations which provide nothing but food and accommodation, to others that provide these plus a wage. In general the vast majority of agencies provide pocket money on top of basic accommodation and food.

However there are some that pay a higher wage than many leisure and travel companies. Take care in your selection. A few agencies charge a registration fee and, amazingly, also offer the lowest remuneration.

However there are good established companies such as Voluntary Service Overseas that look after their employees totally, even to the extent of providing expenses for buying clothes that are suitable for the region. A newer, Canadian based, company called Right To Play International recruits volunteers to work throughout Africa and Asia, and pay an honorarium as well as providing ten days' training in Toronto, Canada.

Before volunteering for any project make sure you are clear about how long you want to spend in this type of work, as periods of employment can commit you to working anything from one week to three years.

There are several books in Chapter 9 that go into greater detail if you are interested in pursuing this option.

Advantages to volunteering
- ◆ Knowing that you are doing a job that is really worthwhile.

- ◆ Working in a team with definite objectives.

- ◆ Having the opportunity to see the problems, as well as the sights, of a country at first hand.

- ◆ All the arrangements are made for you.

- ◆ Voluntary work always looks impressive on a CV, so is useful when applying for jobs on return to the UK.

Illustrating recent opportunities

Voluntary Service Overseas has been paying volunteers to work in sports related projects for a long, long time. There have recently, through VSO, been opportunities to work in sport in 30 countries around the world, mainly in Asia and Africa. These positions usually require coaching, teaching and management skills as a prerequisite. Appointments vary in length from two weeks to three years and applicants must be at least 18 years old with practically no upper age limit.

VSO do their utmost to cater for all their volunteers' requirements. All travel arrangements, including visas and work permits, are organised and paid for by them. Before leaving Britain volunteers receive a grant which adequately covers the cost of specialist clothing and equipment needed to work in the chosen country. Another grant is given halfway through the contract. VSO also cover the costs of accommodation, medical and travel insurance, and national insurance contributions. On top of all this VSO give their workers a minimum of three weeks' holiday per year and a salary. This is generally a modest living allowance paid by the employer in that country, which will not be much compared to UK rates, but is normally more than adequate to live on by local standards.

CASE STUDY

Anne is bowled over in Costa Rica

Anne went to Costa Rica as a volunteer with Cross Cultural Solutions. She loved it so much that she wrote this account:

'If I had to describe my overall experience in two words, it would be challenging and so worth it (okay that's four words!). It's been almost a month and a half since I came home, and I'm still finding it difficult to put the experience into words. Not because there isn't that much to say but because there is so much to say. I will say that it was definitely one of those experiences in which the whole is greater than the sum of its parts. There were fun parts, challenging parts, sobering parts, frustrating parts. It's so clichéd to say that this "changed my life" but I feel like it enriched my life in ways I'm still discovering. The most prominent thought in my mind as I was preparing to leave and in the days after I returned home was "I need to do this again".'

CAMP COUNSELLING AND SUMMER CAMPS

Summer camps are now common around the world, but started in North America, which is still the place that they are predominantly found. There are over 12,000 of them throughout the whole of the USA. Several holiday companies now run their own camps in various countries, but the biggest names in this field, BUNAC and Camp America, still operate mainly in the USA. Between them they offer sports-related work in:

aerobics	karate
archery	lacrosse
athletics (track and field)	life saving
baseball	motorboating
basketball	rifle shooting
camping*	rock climbing
canoeing**	rollerblading

cycling	sailing
diving	soccer
fencing	swimming
golf	tennis
gymnastics	volleyball
hiking	waterskiing
hockey	weight training
horse riding	windsurfing
judo	

*Camping offers other specialisms: outdoor cooking, campcraft and ropes courses.

**Canoeing offers other specialisms of kayaking and expeditions.

To help you with your decision making a list of what both Camp America and BUNAC offer is included below.

◆ Orientation training before commencing work.

◆ Arranging work permits and visas.

◆ Return airfare and transfers to and from your camp.

◆ Food and accommodation.

◆ A basic salary.

◆ Six or seven weeks' holiday time, after camp, before returning to your own country.

BUNAC

BUNAC stands for British Universities North America Club and they arrange employment at summer camps in the USA and Canada. Since their inauguration in 1962 they have now branched out to arrange work in many other countries, but most of this is of the non-sporting type. More information is available on their website – details in Chapter 9.

BUNAC charge a registration fee (refundable if your application is unsuccessful), and a membership fee, if you obtain work through them. In addition you will have to pay for:

1. Travel to your interview and orientation (at a university near you).
2. Your own medical.
3. Your own visa.
4. Medical, accident and baggage insurance.

Rates of pay vary and you are advised to establish your remuneration before accepting your appointment.

Camp America
Camp America have been running summer camps for more than 30 years. They don't organise work outside the USA, but they do offer a wider range of sporting activities. Interviews are held all over the UK, so if you reach that stage you will not have too far to travel. You will not be required to undergo a medical examination, but you will have to complete a medical form. If you are given a placement you will need to get confirmation of your medical history from your doctor, who will also have to confirm your suitability for the programme. These costs are met by you. At your interview you will have to pay a first deposit, followed by a second payment if you obtain a placement. This, however, covers your visa fee and airport taxes.

The amount of 'wage' that you receive depends on your age, type of job and experience. See their website – details in Chapter 9 – for more information.

Looking at other camps around the world

Following the American example summer camps and activity holidays have become popular in many other countries and the majority of these are organised for children. Brochures are not easy to come by as the majority of companies specialising in these holidays mail direct to schools. So ask your local P.E. teacher if they have any spare copies, as well as enquiring at your local travel agents and take your contact addresses from these. Sometimes you can find adverts for this type of holiday in national newspapers as well.

Finally, unless you have the website address of companies such as PGL, you could try a general search through one of the internet search engines like MSN, Google, etc for summer camps – there are literally thousands of entries.

CASE STUDY

A great experience and a great holiday too!

Karen was in her second year of teacher training when some friends suggested financing a holiday in America by working in a summer camp through BUNAC.

She went through all the formalities: interview, medical, etc, before being employed as a tennis coach at Kenwood Camp in Connecticut.

After working at the summer school Karen took time out to tour around the States, taking in such attractions as the Statue of Liberty, Grand Canyon and of course Disneyland.

Karen enjoyed her time there so much that she returned to work there the following year, but this time in the higher paid job of Group Leader, which meant being responsible for 22 11-year-old children.

Only family circumstances prevented Karen from going back for a third term. She said that 'working with BUNAC has been an important part of my life. I really enjoyed the work. It also assisted in financing my tour of the States. I could not have afforded to see the Grand Canyon and other sights without it.

I am positive that having this on my CV also helped me to secure my current teaching post.'

TAKING A YEAR (OR MORE) OUT

If past experiences are borne out, most people reading this book will be either school leavers or studying at university, or just graduated, and who would like to see a bit more of the world before settling into a career.

This is not a bad idea. Many people, including future employers, think that a break from the education system not only helps you to apply yourself to future studies, but also that you will be a more mature, capable person as a result of your experiences.

Sometimes taking a year out can change your career plan and you might decide against going back to college in the immediate future. All the options listed in this book are ideal ways for you to gain employment, but the seasonal and voluntary work sections should be of particular relevance. However if you are considering this, but would like more information, there are several books on the subject listed in Chapter 9. Many of these will be stocked at your main library.

CASE STUDY

Simon makes a career change
Simon was nearing the end of his electrical engineering degree at Sheffield University and was considering taking a year out when his phone rang. His older sister, who was already working in Thailand, told him about an opportunity that had become available as a swimming instructor. She knew that Simon was already qualified in this area and it seemed ideal for him. Without hesitation, after term had finished Simon headed for Bangkok. He thoroughly enjoyed his work there and stayed well beyond his year out. He gained promotion and moved up to being the manager of all the hotel's leisure facilities which included tennis coaching, aerobics, weight training, etc.

He is now manager of all leisure provision within the hotel group, responsible for the whole region between Hong Kong and Thailand!

STUDYING WHILST COACHING AND COMPETING

Sports scholarships started in the USA, but have since spread to all corners of the globe. Much of the USA's sporting success was, and still is, college based. Now many other nations are trying to emulate this success by adopting the same system of offering cash incentives to the more gifted sportspeople to study at their institutions.

Although there are increasing opportunities to gain sports scholarships worldwide, the vast majority are still in American colleges – but Britain is rapidly catching up.

The National Collegiate Athletic Association (NCAA) has strict rules about when students can be signed to American college teams – so check on this before applying – the situation, however, is more relaxed in Britain.

Gaining a sports scholarship at a university has three major advantages.

1. It is a great way of playing and improving your sport.

2. Trying to compete at sport whilst holding down a full-time job often leaves you jaded and your performance suffers.

3. Once qualified many employers find this, plus your skill and experience, ideally suitable for their company.

Coaching opportunities

If your forte is coaching you could work within the college system by applying for a postgraduate 'assistantship'. As the title suggests you would apply to work as an assistant coach for one of the college teams and in return you receive your postgraduate tuition and accommodation free of charge. This not only enables you to come out with a higher level degree, but also gives you valuable contacts within the system which may eventually lead to further opportunities.

Most of these assistantship opportunities exist in American universities, but more and more are now appearing in the UK and other parts of the world. Traditionally, if you wanted to pursue this option, you contacted your chosen university direct. This is still viable, but now an increasing number of colleges are advertising these posts on the internet. See Chapter 5 for British universities addresses.

Avoiding the pitfalls

If these opportunities look enticing and desirable you should heed a few words of warning. Whilst the vast majority of students returning to the UK, after completing an assisted course, recount their wonderful experiences, there have also been a small number of horror stories. Some students have returned, often without completing their course, because of the excessive pressure they were under from the college's head coach. They have complained about such things as being asked to compete whilst still injured, or to take on different roles within their sport than they are used to. For example, being accepted as a high jumper but being coerced into competing as a javelin thrower or steeplechaser to gain valuable points for their college team. Noncompliance with the coach's request is often then followed by the threat of withdrawal of the student's funding.

This is a case of 'he who pays the fiddler calls the tune' and can be understandable when the coach themself is under enormous pressure to produce results. However, it must be pointed out that this is not the norm. The majority of coaches conduct themselves in a totally professional manner.

The best way to avoid problems is to extensively research your preferred college, also, if finances permit, to visit it and talk to the coaching staff and students. It is worth noting, however, that you are less likely to be used as a dogsbody the more valuable you are to them. In other words the higher standard you compete at means the more likely they are to look after your welfare.

If your chosen path is to apply to American colleges then an absolutely invaluable book to consult is *Sports Scholarships and College Programs in the USA*. It comprehensively covers all aspects of sports scholarships in the States and you can find more details on it in Chapter 9.

CASE STUDY

Steven makes sacrifices to have a great time abroad

Steven missed his family and friends, fish and chips, curries and the English sense of humour, in order to pursue his dream in the USA.

He had been inspired to try for a golf scholarship when he was at a tournament in Aberystwyth and met a fellow competitor who had just completed his American degree by this method. So Steven sent his CV to several colleges. Fortunately Campbell University in North Carolina picked him up.

Steven absolutely loved it. It was hard work sometimes juggling classes and training and competing. Golf took up so much time, not like soccer where training would last a couple of hours, and competition 90 minutes. Qualifying rounds in tournaments could last five and a half hours, and training even longer.

All in all though Steven feels fortunate to have been given this opportunity to gain a qualification – he came out with a Master Degree in Business Administration – whilst experiencing a different culture, visiting places that he'd only seen on TV, *and* improving at the sport that he loved.

For a short time Steven worked as an assistant golf coach, whilst he was studying for his Masters, but as soon as he qualified moved into a job that he describes as spectacular. He is now the UK Marketing Director for Disney on Ice.

He says: 'every day is different, challenging and rewarding. I get the opportunity to do some pretty spectacular things for special people. Seeing kids' excitement when they meet Mickey Mouse or their favourite Disney character is priceless.'

WORKING IN SPORTS RELATED EMPLOYMENT

There are numerous jobs closely connected with sport that could also give rise to employment abroad. They might not involve you directly with your own sport, but the work may be satisfying merely through being associated with it. The list of British jobs contained in Chapter 2 is obviously relevant to other countries, but it does have some exceptions. For example, some of the third world countries may not be wealthy enough to employ county development officers.

Opportunities for employment in sports related jobs exist globally, but employers would expect you to have experience in your own country before applying.

If you would like to investigate this option further then refer to Chapters 2 and 4 to help you assess the market and Chapter 6 to identify the qualifications you will need.

WORKING IN CLOSE PROXIMITY TO YOUR SPORT

If you would like to work in a job that keeps you in close proximity to your sport, without actually participating – for example working in a ski resort in a domestic capacity and using your leisure time to ski – then there are countless opportunities for employment.

Leisure is the main worldwide growth industry. Experts estimate that the travel industry in Britain is growing at more than two and a half times that of GNP (gross national product).

Many leisure companies employ thousands of workers both in Britain and abroad and the internet regularly advertises opportunities for these. Apart from leisure companies, there are many other employers out there who not only advertise on the internet but also in specialist career-related magazines like *The Lady* (for domestic employment), *The Stage* (for entertainers), *Nursing Times*, etc.

Finding the right job for yourself
Holiday companies in particular require people to work as:

accounts clerk	dishwasher
administrative assistant	driver
airport rep	electrician
babysitter	entertainment organiser
bar staff	fibre-glasser
beautician	fire safety officer
boiler technician	groundsman
boat maintenance	group leader
bus driver/staff	hairdresser
campsite courier	handyman
campsite services attendant	holiday rep
carpenter	instructor
centre manager	interpreter
chalet maid	janitor
chambermaid	kindergarten teacher
coffee bar staff	manager
cook/kitchen assistant	mechanic
courier	musician
croupier	nanny

night auditor	sewing machinist
nurse	shipping clerk
office staff	shop worker
painter	ski lift attendant
photographer	ski lift mechanic
plumber	ski technician
porter	store assistant
printer	teacher
receptionist	telephone operator
rescue boat personnel	ticket collector
rodent control officer	tour guide
service station staff	waiter/waitress

Working in the leisure industry

If you want to pursue this option make sure you apply at the right time. Most leisure companies start recruiting for their winter season between April and August. However, in the past there have still been a limited number of vacancies available in the autumn, so you could still be lucky.

Companies requiring summer workers generally accept applications between September and February, but again applicants have been successful as late as April.

Obviously, in all cases the earlier you apply the more choice you have and the greater your chances of success.

If you don't necessarily want to work in a job connected with your sport, but merely want to be close to the facilities that you need, the opportunities are endless. Many newspapers, magazines and the internet carry adverts from employers abroad asking for British men and women to work for them.

This can be a good way to earn some money and enjoy your sport, because this option has several advantages over other types of work.

◆ You are still fresh and keen for your sport when you have finished your daily job.

◆ If you have selected wisely, you are close to your sport's arena.

◆ You are surrounded by like-minded people.

In other categories of sports related work many people become disillusioned when they realise that they have no time or energy to participate, having spent all day coaching/teaching it.

You can find some examples of past opportunities under Employment in Close Proximity to Your Sport in Chapter 4, and more ideas can be formulated from the list of journals in Chapter 9.

CASE STUDY

Ollie – what an incredible character
Ollie always wanted to be in the leisure/entertainment industry. He was German Masters Champion at table tennis in 1998 and now coaches this plus volleyball, pool and many other sports as Chief Entertainments Officer at Palm Oasis in Gran Canaria.

When I asked him what qualifications he needed for the job he replied 'None really, just a good all round ability in sport and entertaining.'

He certainly has this.

At 15 years of age he left school to study magic at college in Germany for three years. Then he went to San Francisco for a further six months advanced course. As well as these skills he also plays the guitar, piano, saxaphone, flute and clarinet, and is fluent in German, English and Spanish, but says that he can only just get by in Italian and Dutch.

Ollie eventually worked his way up to this job, having first worked as a waiter in Holland, then with Eurocamp in Italy, before working in another resort in Gran Canaria.

He advises anybody wanting similar work to gain as many skills and qualifications as they can before applying, but mainly to work on their language skills.

THE ARMED FORCES

As with Britain, opportunities exist to pursue your sport whilst employed in the Armed Forces of a foreign country. It is extremely rare for a British national to do this, but there are cases of sportspeople doing so. In recent years Steve Tunstall, who was a GB cross country and track international, served his time in the French Foreign Legion.

If you are interested in pursuing this outlet you should contact the appropriate embassy. The majority of these are located in London and their details can be found in the London telephone directory (copies are normally stored at main libraries) or on the internet.

SELF-ASSESSMENT EXERCISE

1. Which option for using your sport most appeals to you?

2. Do you have the required level of skill and qualifications to enable you to use your sport?

3. Do you know who to contact to pursue your chosen option?

4. Have you decided which country you want to work in?

5. Can you speak the language?

6. Are you prepared to learn the language?

(4)

Finding Employment

ACCESSING THE INFORMATION

The first edition of this book recorded that adverts for employment could be found predominantly in books, magazines, newspapers, sports clubs, sports centres and job centres, as well as on the internet. Whilst these sources are still prominent today, the internet now outstrips the others by far and has become the main source for sports employment opportunities.

Most national organising bodies now have their own website (see Chapter 5 for details) and the majority of these detail employment within their organisation. There are literally *too many* jobs to list them all in this book, so check these websites first.

The internet also contains numerous sites that detail a wealth of employment opportunities. The majority of contact information is free, but there are some agencies that charge a fee for their service. So check out the free sites first, then once these have been exhausted think about subscribing to the fee-paying sites.

Some expense, however, may be worthwhile incurring, as it could be invaluable to you. Subscribe to a specialist sports magazine, as this is more likely to carry employment adverts that have the most relevance to your circumstances, especially if you don't have the internet to subscribe to an ISP (internet service provider) in order to access the above mentioned wealth of adverts.

If, unfortunately, you can't afford these it is not the end of the world. Ask around your local sports club to see if you can borrow magazines from someone. If that fails, remember that some of the bigger libraries stock the most popular sports magazines in their reference section.

A list of many of the most popular sports magazines is included in Chapter 9.

Accessing the internet

The cheapest way to access the internet is to subscribe to a free ISP. However these tend to be a lot slower than broadband which normally incurs expense. This small expense is often worthwhile, though, as you get faster access and less sites jamming, therefore more are available. If however you don't own a computer, or have this access, ask your friends if any of them are online, or visit your local school or college and ask if you can use their facilities.

Otherwise many libraries now offer free, or cheap, access. Many local libraries charge as little as £0.75 an hour for this provision. Likewise there is now an abundance of internet cafes and cybercafes, which charge from £1 upwards. Someone in one of these institutions is normally available to show you, free of charge, how to access the sites that you need. Look them up in *Yellow Pages* and don't forget to enquire about their charges.

If you would like to be able to do more on the internet, rather than just the basics, there are numerous books, stocked by the vast majority of libraries, on this subject. There is also an abundance of free courses, mainly at your local community colleges where, of course, you will probably also be able to use the internet free of charge.

FINDING YOUR SPORT

There is now an abundance of sports jobs advertised on the internet. You will find the majority of the information listed below comes from that source. I have had to trim this list down considerably, as I collected approximately 400 per cent more sports vacancies than I needed for this book, and all this in just two weeks!

So only a fraction of them are detailed here, as an illustration of the types of jobs previously available, some of the exotic locations you could be working in and the addresses of the companies advertising them.

The list contains opportunities that have been recently advertised in company literature, books, magazines, newspapers, or on the internet. You can find full contact addresses, telephone and fax numbers or internet details in Chapter 9. Please bear in mind that by the time you read this book the vast majority of these jobs will have been taken a long time ago, but it still may be worthwhile contacting the companies to enquire whether new opportunities have become available. Much of the work listed is seasonal, but it is often available every year, and many sportsmen and women return to work for the same company time after time.

For each opportunity listed, the internet address is given in the last column. Contact details of companies that have advertised sports related employment are also given in Chapter 9. Each sport is listed alphabetically, with employers' details, and the location of the job is detailed in the middle column.

The employment available is so varied that differing levels of qualification and experience are required. To avoid wasting your time, check on this before applying.

After the listings of jobs in sport I have also included further details of work which has recently been on offer that may not involve participating or coaching your sport, but which will give you opportunities to participate due to close proximity to it.

Finally, Chapter 9 gives details of numerous books, magazines and newspapers that contain useful information regarding finding employment through sport.

JOBS THAT HAVE RECENTLY BEEN AVAILABLE

Aerobics and fitness

Aerobics instructors	Lanzarote, Canaries	leisureopportunities.co.uk
Aerobics instructors	Across Europe and Egypt	markwarner.co.uk
Aerobics and fitness instructors	Worldwide	clubmedjobs.com
Fitness advisors	London	gumtree.com
Fitness instructor	Cleveland	*Northern Echo* newspaper
Fitness instructors	Bermuda	leisureopportunities.co.uk
Fitness instructors	Hull, Altrincham, Chester	totaljobs.com
Fitness instructors	Greece and Turkey	workthing.com

Fitness and lifestyle advisor	Edinburgh	leisureopportunities.co.uk
Gym instructor	Macclesfield	totaljobs.com
Personal fitness trainer	New York, USA	onlinesports.com
Personal trainer	Birmingham	totaljobs.com
Personal trainer	Agile Fitness, London	gumtree.com
Personal trainer	Europe	firstchoice4jobs.co.uk

American football

Assistant football coach	Florida	coachingvacancies.com
Coaching staff	London, Reading, Kent	bafca.org
Head coaches (cadet and junior)	UK	bafca.org
Offense co-ordinator	Oxford Saints	bafca.org

Angling and fishing

| Fishing Instructors | Ontario, Canada | campwhitepine.com |

Archery

Camp Beaumont	Greater London	adventurejobs.co.uk
Instructors	Worldwide	clubmedjobs.com
Instructors	Britain and abroad	travelclass.co.uk
N.A.D. of archery	Florida, USA	teacharchery.org

Athletics (track and field, cross country)

Assistant track and field coach	Maine, USA	umaine.edu/eo/jobs
Athletics centre supervisors	Uxbridge	leisureopportunities.co.uk
Community sports coach	Surrey	activesurrey.com
Competitions co-ordinator	Wales	ukathletics.net
Education and training manager	Wales	ukathletics.net
Elite sports agency	London	gumtree.com
Head track coach	Michigan	coachingvacancies.com
Performance coaches	Throughout UK	ukathletics.net
Track coach	California	coachingvacancies.com

Badminton

| Badminton development officer | Middlesex | sportengland.org |
| PGL Young Adventure | Britain, France and Spain | pgl.co.uk |

BEAMISH
THE NORTH OF ENGLAND OPEN AIR MUSEUM

STABLE TECHNICIAN (Groom)
Scale 2/3(Points 11 - 17) £13,854 - £15,825)
Applications are invited for the above post within the Museum's Estates Department.

For this interesting and unique position we are seeking someone with at least three years professional working experience with driving and riding horses and can turn out to a very high standard. Experience with working with a team of carriage horses would be an advantage. It will also be necessary to communicate with visitors and groups to the museum in a pleasant and courteous manner.

Job description, person specification and application form are available from our website or by contacting:

BEAMISH, The North of England Open Air Museum, Beamish, Co. Durham, DH9 0RG.
Tel: 0191 370 4000   Fax: 0191 370 4001
Email: office@beamish.org.uk   Website: www.beamish.org.uk

Closing date for receipt of completed applications is: 27th October, 2006
Those shortlisted only will be contacted by:10th November, 2006

Beamish is an Equal Opportunities employer and welcomes applications from all sections of the community.
The Museum operates a No Smoking Policy

REGIONAL DEVELOPMENT OFFICER
EASTERN REGION

This temporary position is to cover maternity leave from 1 January 2007

This role requires experience of affiliated dressage and a flexible approach to working 21 hours a week from home. The successful applicant must have their own car, computer and access to email.

They will be involved in the co-ordination of affiliated competition days and venues in the region as well as developing and administering regional judge training, BYRDS activity and regional training.

Please send CV by 20 October 2006 to: Mr David Holmes, Chief Executive, British Dressage, National Agricultural Centre, Stoneleigh Park, Kenilworth, Warwickshire, CV8 2RJ Tel: 024 76 698843
Email: DavidHolmes@britishdressage.co.uk

BRUSSELS BARBARIANS
Founded 1968
www.brusselsbarbarians.com

We seek new players to join us in the Belgian Championship Elite Division and enjoy life in the capital of Europe.

Possible job opportunities for new graduates in EU affairs, plus contract positions for experienced IT Consultants.

Contact: Stuart Dowsett, President
email: rugby@eurocity.be
Tel: 00 32 475 701782

SOCCER COACH
★ USA ★

Ever thought of doing a spot of soccer coaching in the USA? There are hundreds of opportunities available right now to work as soccer coaches in the States. These positions, open to all ages and abilities, offer a lucrative expenses paid trip to the States to coach childrens soccer and most jobs involve only 3 hours work a day! Accommodation is free and you will also have a company car at your disposal. Soccer is booming in America and this is a fantastic opportunity that should not be missed!!!

For more info, please send a S.A.E. to:
Soccer Coach USA, Dept HM, Delta House, 8 Douglas Gs, Durham, DH1 3PT
or go to: www.soccer-coaching-jobs.com

Fig. 4. Examples of the sort of job advertisements you might see in magazines.

Basketball

Basketball instructors	Ontario, Canada	campwhitepine.com
Community sports coach	Surrey	activesurrey.com
Elite Sports Agency	London	gumtree.com
Gap Sports Abroad	S Africa, Ghana, Costa Rica	globalchoices.co.uk
Head basketball coach	Florida	coachingvacancies.com
Land sports organiser	Worldwide	clubmedjobs.com

Boxing

Gap Sports Abroad	S Africa, Ghana, Costa Rica	globalchoices.co.uk

Camping

Acorn Adventure	UK	adventurejobs.co.uk
Alan Rodgers Direct	Europe	markhammerton.com
Backroads	Worldwide	backroads.com
Campsite representative	France	ianmearnsholidays.co.uk
Canvas Holidays	Throughout Europe	canvasholidays.co.uk
Eurocamp	Throughout Europe	eurocamp.co.uk
Keycamp Holidays	Throughout Europe	www2.keycamp.co.uk
Mont/demontage assistants	France	ianmearnsholidays.co.uk

Canoeing (kayaking and rafting)

Acorn Adventure	UK, France and Italy	adventurejobs.co.uk
Backroads	Worldwide	backroads.com
Canoe/kayak instructors	USA	bunac.org.uk
Canoeing instructors	Cumbria and Lancs	workthing.com
Canoeing instructors	Ontario, Canada	campwhitepine.com
Club Med	Worldwide	clubmedjobs.com
Headwater Holidays	Throughout Europe	headwater.com
Mark Warner	Europe and Egypt	markwarner.co.uk
PGL Young Adventure	Britain, France and Spain	pgl.co.uk
Watersports instructor	France and Spain	workthing.com
Watersports instructor	USA (summer camp)	workthing.com

Caving

PGL Young Adventure	Britain, France and Spain	spgl.co.uk

Climbing (see rock climbing and abseiling)

Cricket

Elite Sports Agency	London	gumtree.com
Gap Sports Abroad	S Africa, Ghana,	
	Costa Rica	globalchoices.co.uk
PGL Young Adventure	Britain, France and Spain	pgl.co.uk
Player/coach	Perthshire, Scotland	gumtree.com
Private school cricket coach	London	gumtree.com

Cycling and mountain biking

Backroads	Worldwide	backroads.com
Belle France	France	markhammerton.com
Club Med	Worldwide	clubmedjobs.com
Headwater Holidays	Throughout Europe	headwater.com
Mountain biking leaders	Asia and South America	exodus.co.uk
Regional assistant	France	cycling-for-softies.co.uk
National development coach	Scotland	sportscotland.org.uk
Sunsail	Greece,Turkey	
	and Antigua	globalsuccessor.com

Dance

Community dance/aerobics coach	University of Glos.	jobs.ac.uk
Dance and drama instructor	Home Co. and E. Anglia	workthing.com
Elite Sports Agency	London	gumtree.com
Lecturer of dance	Matthew Boulton College,	
	Birmingham	jobs.ac.uk

Diving (scuba and snorkelling)

Club Med	Worldwide	clubmedjobs.com
Diving instructors	Egypt	emperordivers.com
Watersports instructor	France and Spain	workthing.com

Equestrianism

Horse riding instructor	USA (summer camp)	bunac.org.uk
Horse riding instructor	USA (summer camp)	workthing.com
Horseback riding instructors	Ontario, Canada	campwhitepine.com
PGL Young Adventure	Britain	pgl.co.uk
Ranchexperience	Argentina	globalchoices.co.uk

Fencing

Club Med	Europe and North Africa	clubmedjobs.com
Mark Warner	Europe and North America	markwarner.co.uk

Fishing (see angling)

Football (see American football or soccer)

Golf

Club Med	Worldwide	clubmedjobs.com
Community golf coach	University of Gloucester	jobs.ac.uk
General manager – golf clubs	Essex, Sussex, Staffs, Kent	totaljobs.com
Golf instructors	Lanzarote, Canaries	leisureopportunities.co.uk
Golf instructors	USA (summer camp)	workthing.com
Head golf coach	Florida	coachingvacancies.com
Regional development officer	South West England	sportengland.org

Gymnastics

Elite Sports Agency	London	gumtree.com
Gymnastics instructors	USA (summer camp)	workthing.com
National schools games co-ordinator	British gymnastics Lilleshall, Shrops	
Regional development officer	London and Yorkshire	british gymnastics

Hiking (see walking)

Hockey

Assistant hockey coach	Florida	coachingvacancies.com
Community hockey coach	University of Glos.	jobs.ac.uk

Community sports coach	Surrey	activesurrey.com
Elite Sports Agency	London	gumtree.com
Gap Sports Abroad	S Africa, Ghana, Costa Rica	globalchoices.co.uk
Hockey development officer	Elmbridge, Surrey	activesurrey.com
Performance administrator	Scotland	scottish-hockey.org.uk
Proactive education	Croydon	gumtree.com

Horse riding (see equestrianism)

Ice hockey

Assistant ice hockey coach	Texas	coachingvacancies.com

Ice skating

Queens Icebowl	London	gumtree.com

Kayaking (see canoeing)

Lacrosse

Assistant lacrosse coach	Florida	coachingvacancies.com
Head lacrosse coach	Philadelphia	coachingvacancies.com

Mini motorsports

Camp Beaumont (quadbike instr.)	Across London	adventurejobs.co.uk
Race director (karting)	Daytona, Manchester	manchesteronline.co.uk
Track staff (karting)	Daytona, Manchester	manchesteronline.co.uk

Netball

Active Planet	London	gumtree.com
Community sports coach	Surrey	activesurrey.com
Elite Sports Agency	London	gumtree.com
Head coach	Samuel Marsden Coll., NZ	collegesport.org.nz
Netball development officer	Elmbridge, Surrey	activesurrey.com
School/club links manager	Hitchin	sportengland.org

Orienteering

Instructors	Bury, Lancs.	burrs.org.uk

Rafting (see canoeing)

Rambling (see walking)

Rock climbing and abseiling

Acorn Adventure senior instructors	France and Italy	adventurejobs.co.uk
Climbing instructor	Worldwide	clubmedjobs.com
Climbing Instructor	Cumbria and Lancs	workthing.com
Instructors	Britain and abroad	travelclass.co.uk
PGL Young Adventure	Britain	pgl.co.uk
Resident high ropes director	Illinois, USA	ymcacampduncan.org

Rowing

Part time coaches of juniors	UK	sportengland.org
Performance coach	Adaptive Boats – UK	sportengland.org
Rowing coach	Burway, Surrey	activesurrey.com

Rugby League

Club coach	Harlequins, Surrey	activesurrey.com
Match officials	UK	sportengland.org
Match officials appointment officer	UK	sportengland.org

Rugby Union

Community rugby coach (girls)	University of Gloucester	jobs.ac.uk
Community sports coach	Surrey	activesurrey.com
Elite Sports Agency	London	gumtree.com
Gap Sports Abroad	S Africa, Ghana, Costa Rica	globalchoices.co.uk
Rugby development officer	South Yorkshire	sportengland.org

Sailing

Captains	Worldwide	yachtcrewregister.com

Club Med	Worldwide	clubmedjobs.com
Crystal Holidays	Corsica, Turkey	crystalholidays.co.uk
Deckhands	Worldwide	yachtcrewregister.com
Engineers	Worldwide	yachtcrewregister.com
Flotilla skippers	Greece and Med.	anyworkanywhere.com
Head sailing coach	California	coachingvacancies.com
Jubilee Sailing Trust	Caribbean, Canaries, UK	globalchoices.co.uk
Mark Warner	Europe and Egypt	markwarner.co.uk
PGL Young Adventure	Britain, France and Spain	pgl.co.uk
Sailing instructors	USA (summer camp)	workthing.com
Senior instructors	France, Italy, UK	adventurejobs.co.uk
Sunsail	Greece,Turkey and Antigua	globalsuccessor.com
Watersports instructor	France and Spain	workthing.com
Watersports instructor	USA (summer camp)	workthing.com

Self defence (judo/karate/wrestling etc)

Community martial arts coach	University of Gloucester	jobs.ac.uk
Head wrestling coach	Colorado	coachingvacancies.com
Martial arts instructors	USA (summer camp)	workthing.com
National development officer	Scotland	judoscotland.com
Club Med	Worldwide	clubmedjobs.com

Skateboarding (and in-line skating)

| Club Med | Worldwide | clubmedjobs.com |

Skiing and snowboarding

Alpine Meadows ski resort	USA (instructors)	skialpine.com
Cordon Rouge	Courchevel and Val Thorens	payaway.co.uk
Head alpine ski coach	Maine, USA	umfk.maine.edu
Head assistant ski coach	Florida, USA	coachingvacancies.com
Headwater Holidays (x/c)	Throughout Europe	headwater.com
Mark Warner	Worldwide year round	markwarner.co.uk
PGL Ski Europe	Europe	pgl.co.uk
Purple Ski	French Alps	globalchoices.co.uk
Ski lift operators	Canada	owh.co.uk
Ski instructors	Canada	owh.co.uk

| Ski resort snow maker | Canada | owh.co.uk |
| Snowsports development officer | Scottish Highlands | snowsportscotland.org |

Soccer

Active Planet	London	gumtree.com
Assistant soccer coach	Texas	coachingvacancies.com
Assistant women's soccer coach	North Carolina	collegesportscareers.com
Community sports coach	Surrey	activesurrey.com
Director of athletic (soccer)	Maine University, USA	umfk.maine.edu/jobs
First Choice	Europe	firstchoice4jobs.co.uk
Football coach	Darlington College	darlington.ac.uk
Football development for deaf	Birmingham or London	sportengland.org
Gap Sports Abroad	S Africa, Ghana,	
	Costa Rica	globalchoices.com
Head soccer coach	Florida	coachingvacancies.com
Land sports organiser	Worldwide	clubmedjobs.com
Male and female coaches	USA	ultimatesoccer.org
Soccer coaches	USA	soccer-coching-jobs.com
Soccer instructors	USA	BUNAC
Soccer instructors	USA	workthing.com

Squash

| Club coach | Esporta, Croydon | activesurrey.com |
| Squash instructors | Lanzarote, Canaries | leisureopportunities.co.uk |

Surfing (and wakeboarding)

| Mark Warner | Europe and Egypt | markwarner.co.uk |
| PGL Young Adventure | Britain | pgl.co.uk |

Swimming and lifesaving

Alton Towers, trainee lifeguard	Staffordshire	totaljobs.com
Assistant swimming teacher	Reigate, Surrey	gumtree.com
Camp Beaumont	Across London	adventurejobs.co.uk
Club Med	Worldwide	clubmedjobs.com
Disability coach	Guildford, Surrey	activesurrey.com
First Choice	Europe	firstchoice4jobs.co.uk

In2Action	Spain, Canaries, Turkey	adventurejobs.co.uk
Lifeguard	Woking, Surrey	gumtree.com
RAC and hotels	London	gumtree.com
Resident camp pool director	Illinois, USA	ymcacampduncan.org
Splash	London, Greece and Turkey	gumtree.com
Sportsweb Recruitment Group	Leicester	totaljobs.com
Swimming instructor	Britain	pgl.co.uk
Swimming instructor	USA	BUNAC
Volunteer development manager	Scotland	scottishswimming.com

Table tennis

| Land sports organiser | Worldwide | clubmedjobs.com |

Tennis

Amida Racquets and Fitness	Twickenham	gumtree.com
Club Med	Worldwide	clubmedjobs.com
Elite Sports Agency	London	gumtree.com
First Choice	Europe	firstchoice4jobs.co.uk
Gap Sports Abroad	S Africa, Ghana, Costa Rica	globalchoices.co.uk
Head tennis coach	Texas	coachingvacancies.com
Mark Warner	Across Europe	markwarner.co.uk
Private tennis coach	Chelsea	gumtree.com
Public tennis centre supervisor	London	gumtree.com
Sportsweb Recruitment Group	Leicester	totaljobs.com
Sunsail	Greece, Turkey and Antigua	globalsuccessor.com
Tennis academy coach	Runnymede, Surrey	activesurrey.com
Tennis instructors	Lanzarote, Canaries	leisureopportunities.com

Volleyball (and beach volleyball)

Beach volleyball instructors	Ontario, Canada	campwhitepine.com
Club Med	Worldwide	clubmedjobs.com
Community Volleyball Coaches	Devon and Kent	volleyballengland.org

Walking, hiking and rambling

Backroads	Worldwide	backroads.com
Belle France	France	markhammerton.com
Crystal Holidays	Switzerland and Europe	crystalholidays.co.uk
Headwater Holidays	Throughout Europe	headwater.com
Lead ramblers	Europe and beyond	ramblersholidays.co.uk
Mountain walks organiser	Worldwide	clubmedjobs.com
Swiss Travel Service	Switzerland	globalchoices.co.uk
Trekking leaders	Asia and South America	exodus.co.uk

Waterskiing

Club Med	Worldwide	clubmedjobs.com
Mark Warner	Europe and Egypt	markwarner.co.uk
Sunsail	Greece, Turkey and Antigua	globalsuccessor.com
Waterskiing instructor	USA (summer camp)	workthing.com
Waterskiing instructor	Ontario, Canada	campwhitepine.com

Weight training

Strength coach	Florida	coachingvacancies.com

Windsurfing

Crystal Holidays	Corsica, Turkey	crystalholidays.co.uk
Mark Warner	Europe and Egypt	markwarner.co.uk
PGL Young Adventure	Britain, France and Spain	pgl.co.uk
Sunsail	Greece, Turkey and Antigua	globalsuccessor.com
Watersports instructor	France and Spain	workthing.com
Windsurf instructors	Lanzarote, Canaries	leisureopportunities.co.uk
Windsurf instructors	Ontario, Canada	campwhitepine.com
Windsurf instructors	France	clubmedjobs.com

Yoga

Mark Warner	Europe and Egypt	markwarner.co.uk

EMPLOYMENT IN CLOSE PROXIMITY TO YOUR SPORT

Accounting (auditing)

Crystal Holidays	France, USA	crystalholidays.co.uk
PGL Young Adventure	Britain, France and Spain	pgl.co.uk

Activity organiser

Camp Duncan	Illinois USA	ymcacampduncan.org/jobs
Children's activity assistants	Lanzarote, Canaries	leisureopportunities.co.uk
Group leaders	Cumbria and Lancs	workthing.com
In2Action	Spain, Canaries, Turkey	adventurejobs.co.uk
JCA	South West	adventurejobs.co.uk
Mark Warner	Europe and Egypt	markwarner.co.uk
PGL Young Adventure	Britain, France and Spain	pgl.co.uk

Administration

Admin assistant	French Alps	globalchoices.co.uk
Admin staff	Ontario, Canada	campwhitepine.com
Club Med	Worldwide	clubmedjobs.com
Club services administrator	Lincolnshire	englishgolfunion.org
First Choice	Europe	firstchoice4jobs.co.uk
General assistant	French Alps	globalchoices.co.uk
Hotel reservations co-ordinator	UK	halsbury.com

Airport rep

Crystal Holidays	Worldwide	crystalholidays.co.uk

Alpine studies co-ordinators

PGLSki Europe	France and Spain	pgl.co.uk

Bar staff

Club Med	Worldwide	clubmedjobs.com
Crystal Holidays	France	crystalholidays.co.uk
PGL Young Adventure	Britain and France	pgl.co.uk

Beauty therapists

Club Med	Worldwide	clubmedjobs.com
Mark Warner	Worldwide year round	markwarner.co.uk
Sunsail	Palma, Spain	globalsuccessor.com

Cashiers, sales assistants

Club Med	Worldwide	clubmedjobs.com
Golf membership sales consultant	Hertfordshire	totaljobs.com
Golf Society day-sales	Woking, Surrey	totaljobs.com
Salesperson	UK	halsbury.com

Catering (chefs, cooks, and kitchen assistants, etc)

Bay Diving	Mozambique	payaway.co.uk
Club Med	Worldwide	clubmedjobs.com
Cook and chalet assistant	French Pyrenees	exodus.co.uk
Crystal Holidays	Worldwide	crystalholidays.co.uk
Dining room staff	Ontario, Canada	campwhitepine.com
First Choice	Europe	firstchoice4jobs.co.uk
Go Barging	Scottish Highlands	anyworkanywhere.com
Mark Warner	Worldwide	markwarner.co.uk
PGL Young Adventure	Britain, France and Spain	pgl.co.uk
Qualified chefs	French Alps	globalchoices.co.uk

Chalet staff

Chalet maids/helpers	French Alps	globalchoices.co.uk
Chalet representative	Canada	owh.co.uk
Cordon Rouge	Courchevel and Val Thorens	payaway.co.uk
Crystal Holidays	Canada and across Europe	crystalholidays.co.uk
First Choice	Europe	firstchoice4jobs.co.uk

Chamber staff

Crystal Holidays	France	crystalholidays.co.uk

Childcare

Babysitters	Ontario, Canada	campwhitepine.com
Club Med	Worldwide	clubmedjobs.com
Crystal Holidays	Austria, France, Ibiza, Italy	crystalholidays.co.uk
First Choice	Europe	firstchoice4jobs.co.uk
Sunsail	Greece, Turkey and Antigua	globalsuccessor.com

Circus school

Club Med	Worldwide	clubmedjobs.com

Computers and information technology

PGL Young Adventure	Britain, France and Spain	pgl.co.uk

Dieticians

Club Med	Worldwide	clubmedjobs.com

Driving

(Companies often require HGV or PSV licence and ability to cope with breakdowns)

Drivers	French Alps	globalchoices.co.uk
Drivers	Scottish Highlands	anyworkanywhere.com
Expedition drivers	Africa, Asia and S. America	payaway.co.uk
Overland expedition leaders	Asia and South America	exodus.co.uk

Entertainers

(includes a variety of professions. eg actors, dancers, magicians, musicians, etc. Companies often require previous experience in these positions, and sometimes the ability to speak the local language)

Crystal Holidays	Mediterranean resorts	crystalholidays.co.uk
Club Med	Worldwide	clubmedjobs.com
Entertainment manager	Lanzarote, Canaries	leisureopportunities.co.uk
First Choice	Europe	firstchoice4jobs.co.uk

Fire safety officers

Senior firefighter	Grand Canyon, USA	usajobs.opm.gov

First aiders, health work

Resident camp health officer	Illinois, USA	ymcacampduncan.org
SportHealth project coordinators	E.Chad and Mozambique	sportengland.org

Groundsman (groundskeeper)

Assistant groundsman	London	gumtree.com
Groundsman	Taunton, Somerset	totaljobs.com
Head course ranger	Jersey, C.I.	lamoyegolfclub.co.uk
Seasonal greenkeeper	Cleveland	*Northern Echo* newspaper

Hairdressers

Club Med	Worldwide	clubmedjobs.com
Mark Warner	Worldwide year round	markwarner.co.uk

Hotel work

Crystal Holidays	Worldwide	crystalholidays.co.uk
Mark Warner	Worldwide (year round)	markwarner.co.uk

Housekeeping

Crystal Holidays	Worldwide	crystalholidays.co.uk
Laundry staff	Ontario, Canada	campwhitepine.com

Language teaching

PGL Young Adventure	Britain, France and Spain	pgl.co.uk

Lecturers, etc

Assoc. lecturer in sport	Henley College, UK	henleycol.ac.uk
Lecturer in community sport	University of Greenwich	jobs.ac.uk
Lecturer in sport and exercise sci	Massey University, NZ	jobs.ac.uk
Lecturer in sports and ex. physiology	University of Gloucester	jobs.ac.uk
Lecturer in sports rehabilitation	University of Bolton	jobs.ac.uk
Lecturer in sports science	University of Essex	jobs.ac.uk
Lecturer in sports studies	University of Central Lancs	jobs.ac.uk
Professor & Dean Sch. of Phys Ed.	University of Otago, NZ	jobs.ac.uk

Professor in p. activity and public		
Hlth	University of Gloucester	jobs.ac.uk
Professor of Sport and Exercise		
Sci	Heriot-Watt University, Scotland	jobs.ac.uk
Sports Scientist	Lancashire	leisureopportunities.co.uk

Leisure Centres

Leisure centre assistant manager	Hounslow	totaljobs.com
Leisure club managers	London, Kent, Glos	leisureopportunities.co.uk
Recreation assistants	Middlesex	totaljobs.com

Maintenance staff

Cordon Rouge	Courchevel and Val Thorens	payaway.co.uk
Maintenance staff	Ontario, Canada	campwhitepine.com
Maintenance worker	Grand Canyon, USA	usajobs.opm.gov
PGL Young Adventure	Britain, France and Spain	pgl.co.uk
Sunsail	Greece,Turkey	
	and Antigua	globalsuccessor.com

Management

Acorn Adventure (Watersports)	UK, France amd Italy	adventurejobs.co.uk
Ass. sports development officer	Northants	leisureopportunities.co.uk
Bar managers	Worldwide	crystalholidays.co.uk
Campsite area managers	France	ianmearnsholidays.co.uk
Catering manager	France	crystalholidays.co.uk
Chalet and ski managers	France	crystalholidays.co.uk
Club manager	Edinburgh	leisureopportunities.co.uk
Club Med	Worldwide	clubmedjobs.com
Contracts manager	Italy	crystalholidays.co.uk
Cordon Rouge	Courchevel and Val Thorens	payaway.co.uk
David Lloyds Leisure	Manchester	manchesteronline.co.uk
Gym manager	London	gumtree.com
Hotel manager	Andorra	crystalholidays.co.uk
Mark Warner (beach manager)	Abu Soma, Egypt	markwarner.co.uk
PGL Young Adventure	Britain, France and Spain	pgl.co.uk
Reservations/ops manager		
– skiing	London	totaljobs.com

Sales managers – Golf	Sussex, Hampshire, Essex	totaljobs.com
Spa managers	Dubai	leisureopportunities.co.uk
Sports officer	Macclesfield	totaljobs.com
Stadium Managers	Qatar	jobsearch.co.uk
Supplies and maintenance manager	French Alps	globalchoices.co.uk
Team manager	Cuba	crystalholidays.co.uk
Waterfront manager	Corsica and Turkey	crystalholidays.co.uk

Miscellaneous others

Assistant tournament director	Dallas, USA	onlinesports.com
Campaign worker (racism in sport)	Glasgow	address in appendix
Primary school sports coaches	Bolton	leisureopportunities.co.uk
Projects (sport) worker	Easington, Durham	sector1.net
Security/crowd control	Dallas, USA	onlinesports.com
Sports sales rep/turnstiles tickets	New Jersey, USA	onlinesports.com
Ushers/ticket takers	Dallas, USA	onlinesports.com

Nannies

Crystal Holidays	Across Europe	crystalholidays.co.uk
Mark Warner	Worldwide year round	markwarner.co.uk
Sunsail	Greece, Turkey and Antigua	globalsuccessor.com

Nurses

Camp White Pine	Ontario, Canada	campwhitepine.com
Club Med	Worldwide	clubmedjobs.com

Pool attendants

Mark Warner	Europe and Egypt	markwarner.co.uk

Porters

Club Med	Worldwide	clubmedjobs.com

Receptionists

Club Med	Worldwide	clubmedjobs.com

Crystal Holidays	France	crystalholidays.co.uk

Resort reps, couriers, etc

Cordon Rouge	Courchevel and Val Thorens	payaway.co.uk
Crystal Holidays	Worldwide	crystalholidays.co.uk
First Choice	Europe	www.firstchoice4jobs.co.uk
PGL Ski Europe	Europe	pgl.co.uk
Representative	Swiss Alps	globalchoices.co.uk
Resort managers	Swiss Alps	globalchoices.co.uk
SkiWorld	Europe	adventurejobs.co.uk

Sports massage (physiotherapists, etc)

Club Med	Worldwide	clubmedjobs.com
Mark Warner	Worldwide year round	markwarner.co.uk
Massage therapists	Knightsbridge	leisureopportunities.co.uk
Massage therapists	Lanzarote, Canaries	leisureopportunities.co.uk
Physiotherapists	Lanzarote, Canaries	leisureopportunities.co.uk
Spa therapists	Cheshire	leisureopportunities.co.uk
Sports massage lecturer	Warwickshire	totaljobs.com

Sports officers, etc

Events Officer	London	gumtree.com
Right To Play intern'l volunteer	Asia and Africa	righttoplay.com
Sports development assistant	Elmbridge, Surrey	activesurrey.com
Sports development officer	Mole Valley, Surrey	activesurrey.com
Sports development officer	Brent, London	leisureopportunities.co.uk
Sports therapist	Darlington College	darlington.ac.uk

Stores assistants

PGL Young Adventure	Britain, France and Spain	pgl.co.uk

Teachers

PGL Young Adventure	Britain, France and Spain	pgl.co.uk

Team leaders

Cordon Rouge	Courchevel and Val Thorens	payaway.co.uk

Tour guides

Club Med	Worldwide	clubmedjobs.com
Sports Tours Consultants	Gloucester and Worcester	totaljobs.com

Transport assistants

Crystal Holidays	France	crystalholidays.co.uk

Waiter/waitressess

Club Med	Worldwide	clubmedjobs.com
Crystal Holidays	France	crystalholidays.co.uk
PGL Young Adventure	Britain, France and Spain	pgl.co.uk

Youth leaders

PGL Young Adventure	Britain, France and Spain	pgl.co.uk

$$\left(5\right)$$

Making Contact

This chapter lists the addresses, telephone numbers and websites of most of the major UK sports governing bodies. It was accurate when going to press, however it is constantly changing with additions, deletions, changes of address, telephone numbers, etc. So if you cannot find your Association here, or cannot access them through the data given, contact the information centre at one of the national governing bodies listed below or contact your local library for information.

If you require a sport that is not listed then either contact UK Sport, 40 Bernard Street, London WC1N 1ST, tel: (020) 7211 5100 for advice, or else enter the name of your sport into one of the internet search engines (MSN, Google, Lycos, etc) on a computer.

CONTACTING YOUR NATIONAL GOVERNING BODY

Sport England, 3rd Floor, Victoria House, Bloomsbury Square, London WC1B 4SE. Tel: 08458 508508. www.sportengland.org

Sports Council for Northern Ireland, Upper Malone Road, Belfast BT9 5LA. Tel: 028 90 381222. www.sportni.net

Sport Scotland, Caledonia House, South Gyle, Edinburgh EH12 9DQ. Tel: (0131) 317 7200. www.sportscotland.org.uk

Sports Council for Wales, Sophia Gardens, Cardiff CF11 9SW. Tel: (029) 2033 8200. www.sports-council-wales.co.uk

Contacting your sport's national governing body

Aerobics and Fitness
Keep Fit Association, Astra House, Suite 1.05, Arklow Road, London SE14 6EB. Tel: (020) 8692 9566. www.keepfit.org.uk

Angling
National Federation of Anglers, National Water Sports Centre, Adbolton Lane, Holme Pierrepont, Nottingham NG12 2LU. Tel: (0115) 981 3535. www.nfadirect.com

Archery
The Grand National Archery Society, Lilleshall National Sports Centre, Nr Newport, Shropshire TF10 9AT. Tel: (01952) 677888. www.gnas.org

Athletics
UK Athletics, Athletics House, Central Boulevard, Blythe Valley Park, Solihull, West Midlands B90 8AJ. Tel: 0870 998 6800. www.ukathletics.net

Badminton
Badminton England, National Badminton Centre, Milton Keynes MK8 9LA. Tel: (01908) 268400. www.badmintonengland.co.uk

Basketball
England Basketball, c/o English Institute of Sport, Coleridge Road, Sheffield S9 5DA. Tel: 0870 77 43 623. www.englandbasketball.com

Billiards (see snooker)

Boxing
British Boxing Board of Control, The Old Library, Trinity Street, Cardiff CF10 1BH. Tel: (029) 20 367000. www.bbbofc.com

Canoeing
British Canoe Union HQ, John Dudderidge House, Adbolton Lane, West Bridgford, Nottingham NG2 5AS. Tel: (0115) 982 1100. www.bcu.org.uk

Caving
British Caving Association, Rock Climbing and Caving Centre, Rock House, Station Hill, Chudleigh, Newton Abbot TQ13 0EE. www.british-caving.org.uk

Cricket
England and Wales Cricket Board, Lord's Cricket Ground, London NW8 8QN. www.ecb.co.uk

Cycling (including BMX and mountain biking)
British Cycling, National Cycling Centre, Stuart Street, Manchester M11 4DQ. Tel: 0870 871 2000. www.britishcycling.org.uk

Equestrianism
The British Horse Society, Stoneleigh Deer Park, Kenilworth, Warks CV8 2XZ. Tel. 08701 201918. www.bhs.org.uk

123 The High Street
Thistown
Yorkshire QE2 6PE
Tel: 0123 456789

28 February 200X

Mr J Newbody
The National Coach
Newsport Headquarters

Dear Mr Anybody,

I am interested in playing newsport in a European country for the coming season and I wondered if you might be able to suggest someone I can contact or advise me on my best course of action.

I have three A levels, one of which is German which I also speak fluently, so my preferred countries are Austria, Germany and Switzerland, but I am happy to apply to other EEC countries as well.

I am 18 years old and for the past two years I have played in the Northern League for Thistown United. Last season I was voted their Most Valued Player.

It is my intention to gain experience whilst working abroad before applying to university to study for a sports science degree.

I would be very grateful for your assistance but if you are unable to help could you please send me the addresses of the newsport governing bodies in Austria, Germany and Switzerland.

Thank you for your assistance.

I look forward to hearing from you.

Yours sincerely,

John Jones

John Jones

Fig. 5. Sample letter to a national governing body.

Fencing
British Fencing Association, 1 Baron's Gate, 33–35 Rothschild Rd, London W4 5HT. Tel: (020) 8742 3032. www.britishfencing.com

Football (see soccer)

Golf
English Golf Union Ltd, The National Golf Centre, Woodhall Spa, Lincs LN10 6PU. Tel: (01526) 354500. www.englishgolfunion.org or Professional Golfers Association www.pga.info

Gymnastics
British Gymnastics, Ford Hall, Lilleshall Sports Centre, Newport, Shrops TF10 9NB. Tel: 0845 1297129. www.british-gymnastics.org

Handball
British Handball Association, 40 Newchurch Road, Rawtenstall, Rossendale, Lancs BB4 7QX. Tel: (01706) 229354. www.britishhandball.com

Hang gliding and paragliding
British Hang Gliding and Paragliding Association Ltd, The Old Schoolroom, Loughborough Road, Leicester LE4 5PJ. Tel: (0116) 261 1322. www. bhpa.co.uk

Hockey
England Hockey, The National Hockey Stadium, Silbury Boulevard, Milton Keynes, MK9 1HA. Tel: (01908) 544644. www.englandhockey.co.uk

Horse riding (see equestrianism)

Ice hockey
Ice Hockey UK, 19 Heather Avenue, Rise Park, Romford, RM1 4SL. Tel: 07917 194 264
www. icehockeyuk.co.uk

Judo
British Judo Association, Suite B, Loughborough Technical Park, Epinal Way, Loughborough LE11 3GE. Tel: (01509) 631670. www. britishjudo.org.uk

Karate
BKA, Clifton Chambers, 2 Clifton Road, Prestwich, Manchester M25 3HQ. Tel: (0161) 773 6456.
www. britishkarateassociation.co.uk

Lacrosse
English Lacrosse Association, 26 Wood Street, Manchester M3 3EF. Tel: (0161) 834 4582.
www. englishlacrosse.co.uk

Modern pentathlon
MPAGB, Norwood House, University of Bath, Claverton Down, Bath BA2 7AY. Tel: (01225) 386808.
www. mpagb.org.uk

Motor sports
The Royal Automobile Club Motor Sports Association Limited, Motor Sports House, Riverside Park, Colnbrook SL3 0HG. Tel: (01753) 765000.
www. msauk.org

Mountain biking (see cycling)

Mountaineering
British Mountaineering Council, 177–179 Burton Road, Manchester M20 2BB. Tel: 0870 0104878.
www. thebmc.co.uk

Netball
England Netball, Netball House, 9 Paynes Park, Hitchin, Herts, SG5 1EH. Tel: (01462) 442344.
www. england-netball.co.uk

Orienteering
British Orienteering Federation, 8a Stancliffe House, Whitworth Road, Darley Dale, Matlock, Derbyshire DE4 2HJ. Tel: (01629) 734042.
www. britishorienteering.org.uk

Parachuting
British Parachute Association, 5 Wharf Way, Glen Parva, Leicester LE2 9TF. Tel: (0116) 278 5271.
www. bpa.org.uk

Pool
BPPPA, 23 Kendal Rd, Stretford Marina, Manchester M32 0DZ. Tel: 07891 149685. www. bpppa.org

Rowing
Amateur Rowing Council, 6 Lower Mall, Hammersmith, London W6 9DJ. Tel: 0870 060 7100.
www. oara-rowing.org

Rugby League
Rugby Football League, Red Hall, Red Hall Lane, Leeds

LS17 8NB. Tel: (0113) 232 9111. www. therfl.co.uk

Rugby Union
Rugby Football Union, Rugby Road, Twickenham, Middlesex TW1 1DS. Tel: (020) 8831 6527. www. rfu.com

Sailing
Royal Yachting Association, Ensign Way, Hamble, Southampton SO31 4YA. Tel: 0845 345 0400. www. rya.org.uk

Skiing and snowboarding
English Ski Council, Area Library Building, Halesowen, West Midlands B63 4AJ. Tel: (0121) 501 2314. www.sports-1-link.co.uk

Snooker and billiards
English Association for Snooker and Billiards, 1st Floor, High Howden Social Club, Tynemouth Road, Howden, Wallsend, Tyne and Wear NE28 0EA. Tel: (0191) 262 4333. www.easb.org

Soccer
(Given this title so not to confuse with American Football, Australian Rules, rugby)
The Football Association, 16 Lancaster Gate, London W2 3LW. Tel: (020) 7745 4999. www. thefa.com

Squash
England Squash, National Squash Centre, Rowsley Street, Manchester M11 3FF. Tel: (0161) 231 4499. www. squash.co.uk

Surfing

British Surfing Association., Fistral Beach, Newquay, Cornwall TR7 1HY. Tel: (01637) 876474. www. britsurf.co.uk

Swimming (life saving listed under National Bodies below)

ASA, Harold Fern House, Derby Square, Loughborough, Leicestershire LE11 5AL. Tel: (01509) 618700. www. britishswimming.org

Table tennis

English Table Tennis Association, 3rd Floor, Queensbury House, Havelock Road, Hastings, East Sussex TN34 1HF. Tel: (01424) 722525. www. englishtabletennis.org.uk

Ten pin bowling

British Ten Pin Bowling Association, 114 Balfour Road, Ilford, Essex IG1 4JD. Tel: (020) 8478 1745. www. btba.org.uk

Tennis

The Lawn Tennis Association, Palliser Road, West Kensington, London W14 9EG. Tel: (020) 7381 7000. www. lta.org.uk

Trampolining (see gymnastics)

Volleyball

English Volleyball Association, Suite B, Loughborough Technology Centre, Epinal Way, Loughborough LE11 3GE. Tel: (01509) 631699. www. volleyballengland.org

Waterskiing

British Water Ski, The Tower, Thorpe Road, Chertsey, Surrey KT16 8PH. Tel: (01932) 575364. www. britishwaterski.org.uk

Weightlifting

BWLA, Lilleshall National Sports Centre, Nr Newport, Shropshire TF10 9AT. Tel: (01952) 604201. www. sports-1-link.co.uk

Windsurfing (see sailing)

NATIONAL ORGANISING BODIES

Association of Chartered Physiotherapists in Sports Medicine, C/o Sandra Barley, 5 Ewden House, 12 Holyrood Avenue, Lodge Moor, Sheffield S10 4NW. Tel: (0114) 230 5665. www.acpsm.org

British Red Cross, UK Office, 44 Moorfields, London EC2Y 9AL. Tel: 0870 1707000. www. redcross.org.uk

British Universities Sports Association, BUSA, 20–24 Kings Bench Street, London SE1 0QX. Tel: (020) 7633 5080. www. busa.org.uk

The Central Council of Physical Recreation, Francis House, Francis Street, London SW1P 1DE. Tel: (020) 7854 8501. www.ccpr.org.uk

The Chartered Society of Physiotherapy, CSP, 14 Bedford Row, London WC1R 4ED. Tel: (020) 7306 6666. www. csp.org.uk

City and Guilds, 1 Giltspur Street, London EC1A 9DD. Tel: (020) 7294 2468. www. city-and-guilds.co.uk

The Institute for Outdoor Learning, The Barn, Plumpton Old Hall, Plumpton, Penrith, Cumbria CA11 9NP. Tel: (01768) 885800. www. outdoor-learning.org

Learn Direct, only able to contact over phone or internet.
Tel: 0800 100 900. www. learndirect.co.uk

Royal Life Saving Society, Lifesavers, River House, High
Street, Broom, Warwickshire B50 4HN. Tel: (01789)
773994. www. lifesavers.org.uk

Sports Coach UK, 114 Cardigan Road, Headingley, Leeds
LS6 3BJ. Tel: (0113) 274 4802.
www. sportscoachuk.org

St John Ambulance Brigade, 27 St. John's Lane, London
EC1M 4BU. Tel: 08700 104950. www. sja.org.uk

You might need to write a letter, as shown in Figure 6, for
one of many reasons. This one is shown as an example of
how to acquire more qualifications.

CONTACTING A BRITISH UNIVERSITY WHICH OFFERS SPORTS SCHOLARSHIPS

An outline of what is on offer is given in more detail in
Chapter 2. Below are the addresses of colleges and
universities that have recently offered sports scholarships
and bursaries.

If you have problems accessing the information you need
contact the British Universities Sports Association at 20–
24 Kings Bench Street, London SE1 0QX, tel: (020) 7633
5080, busa.org.uk for advice.

Aberdeen University, Sport and Recreation Services,
Butchart Recreation Centre, University Road, Aberdeen AB24 3UT. Tel: (01224) 272318.
www.abdn.ac.uk

University of Birmingham, Edgbaston, Birmingham B15
2TT. Tel: (0121) 414 3344. www.bham.ac.uk

123 The High Street
Thistown
Yorkshire QE2 6PE
Tel: 0123 456789

28 February 200X

The British Red Cross
National Headquarters

Dear Sir,

I am interested in taking a course that will lead to becoming qualified in first aid. Unfortunately I haven't been able to obtain this information from either my local library or through local newspapers.

Could you please provide me with the contact address of the local organiser of these courses and, if possible, let me know the dates they run, and the cost of enrolment.

Thank you for your assistance.

I look forward to hearing from you.

Yours sincerely,

John Jones

John Jones

Fig. 6. Sample letter to a national organising body.

Bristol University, Centre for Sport, Exercise and Health , Tyndall Avenue, Bristol BS8 1TP. Tel: (0117) 928 8810. www.bris.ac.uk

Brunel University, School of Sport and Education, Uxbridge, Middlesex UB8 3PH. Tel: (01895) 267156. www.brunel.ac.uk

University of Cambridge, contact addresses available through website. www. cam.ac.uk

Cardiff University, Cardiff, CF10 3XQ. Tel: (029) 2087 4000. www.cardiff.ac.uk

Coventry University, Priory Street, Coventry CV1 5FB. Tel: 024 7688 7688, www.cov.ac.uk

De Montfort University, Scholarships Administrator. The Gateway, Leicester, LE1 9BH. Tel: (0116) 255 1551. www.dmu.ac.uk

Durham University, University Office, Old Elvet, Durham DH1 3HP. Tel: (0191) 334 7123. www.dur.ac.uk

Edinburgh University, Sports Scholarships, Old College, South Bridge, Edinburgh EH8 9YL. Tel: (0131) 650 9664. www.ed.ac.uk

Exeter University, The Queen's Drive, Exeter, Devon EX4 4QJ. Tel: (01392) 661000. www.ex.ac.uk

Glasgow University, Recruitment Admissions and Participation Service, Glasgow G12 8QQ. Tel: thro UCAS on 0870 1122200. www.gla.ac.uk

Heriot-Watt University, Riccarton, Edinburgh EH14 1AS. Tel: (0131) 449 5153. www.hw.ac.uk

Leeds Metropolitan University, Civic Quarter, Leeds LS1 3HE. Tel: (0113) 283 6701. www.lmu.ac.uk

Loughborough University, Sports Development Centre, Loughborough, Leics. LE11 3TU. Tel: (01509) 263171. www. lboro.ac.uk

University of Manchester, Oxford Road, Manchester M13 9PL. Tel: (0161) 306 6000. www.manchester.ac.uk

Newcastle University, Newcastle NE1 7RU. Tel: (0191) 222 6000. www.ncl.ac.uk

University of Northumbria, Sport Northumbria, Northumberland Rd, Newcastle upon Tyne NE1 8ST. Tel: (0191) 227 4195. www.northumbria.ac.uk

Oxford University, need to contact individual colleges. Information on website regarding this. www.ox.ac.uk

Queen's University Belfast, The Admissions Office, Belfast BT7 1NN Northern Ireland. Tel: (028) 9097 5081. www.qub.ac.uk

St. Andrew's University, Admissions Centre, St Katharine's, The Scores, St Andrews, Fife KY16 9AX. Tel: (01334) 462150. www.st-andrews.ac.uk

Stirling University, Department of Sports Studies, Stirling FK9 4LA. Tel: (01786) 466900 or 466924. www.stir.ac.uk

University of Strathclyde, 16 Richmond Street, Glasgow G1 1XQ. Tel: (0141) 552 4400. www.strath.ac.uk

University of Sunderland, Sunderland SR1 3SD. Tel: (0191) 515 2000. www.sunderland.ac.uk

University of Surrey, UniSPORT, Guildford GU2 7XH. Tel: (01483) 300800. www.surrey.ac.uk

Swansea University, Singleton Park, Swansea SA2 8PP. Tel: (01792) 205678. www.swan.ac.uk

University of Teesside, Sport and Recreation Unit, Middlesbrough TS1 3BA. Tel: (01642) 342267. www.tees.ac.uk

University of Ulster, Scheme Administrator, Room 11D08, Shore Rd, Newtownabbey BT37 0QB. Tel: 08700 400 700. www.ulster.ac.uk

University of Wales Aberystwyth, Marketing and Recruitment, Old College, King Street, Aberystwyth SY23 2AX. Tel: (01970) 622065. www.aber.ac.uk
University of Wales Bangor, Gwynedd LL57 2DG. Tel: (01248) 383561. www.bangor.ac.uk
University of Wales Newport, Caerleon Campus, PO Box 101, Newport NP18 3YH. Tel: (01633) 432432. www.newport.ac.uk
University of Worcester, Henwick Grove, Worcester WR2 6AJ. Tel: (01905) 855000. www.worcester.ac.uk

CONTACTING AN OVERSEAS UNIVERSITY OFFERING SPORTS SCHOLARSHIPS

The number of universities and colleges around the world offering sports scholarships is so numerous that to include details of them all would be beyond the scope of this book.

However, information on opportunities in the USA is easily accessed through the numerous search engines, or alternatively by reading *Sports Scholarships and College Programs in the USA*: editor Ron Walker by Petersons Guides. This can be borrowed from most main libraries or purchased from the UK distributor Vacation Work Publications.

Scholarships in other parts of the world are now becoming more abundant and can be easily accessed through the internet. Either type the name of the university or country that you are interested in into a search engine (MSN, Google, Lycos, etc) or table a general request such as 'Sports Scholarships Abroad' and it will come up with an extensive list, mainly of commercial companies that have the required details.

6

Ensuring You Have the Necessary Qualifications

There are no qualifications required for a professional playing career in any sport, just outstanding ability. Unfortunately, though, successful careers can be cut short, at any time, by injury. Bear in mind, also that any sports career that extends beyond seven years is considered to be a long one. It would be foolish therefore to ignore gaining qualifications, or experience, that would assist in developing a new career once the professional sporting one is over. Many soccer clubs acknowledge this and insist that their apprentice professionals study for educational qualifications.

OBTAINING GENERAL QUALIFICATIONS

It is advisable to study for recognised qualifications awarded by reputable bodies. Some of these are detailed below. If you want to pursue a career in coaching or instructing it would be sensible to hold a certificate from your national body. Details of these follow under Acquiring National Coaching Awards.

To gain employment in certain careers you need to study for a certificate or diploma organised by a recognised body within that profession. Details are given below under Gaining Professional Qualifications.

A 'vocational' qualification concentrates on job-related skills and knowledge, compared to an 'academic' qualification which reflects a depth of study in a much narrower subject area.

GCSE

Normally taken when you are at school, so the majority of young people reading this book should already have experience of these and hopefully have gained some passes. However, if you feel that you should have done better, for whatever reason, all is not lost. Most towns have at least one facility where you can resit or even take further examinations. Look them up in *Yellow Pages* under Schools and Colleges.

You may think it is a little unjust, but details of these qualifications will be needed for the rest of your working life. Even when applying for a job aged 50 the employer will ask you what school examination passes you achieved. So it is very important that you do as well as you can in these.

Some of you will have succeeded at GCSE and obtained good grades at 'A' level too. This is an added bonus as more opportunities will be available to you.

Qualifications after you have left school

Once you have left school – with or without GCSEs – there is a whole load of other qualifications that you could obtain, many of them through sports-related courses.

The range and number of these courses can be quite confusing so, in an attempt to simplify them, the following general rules can be applied under the assumption that we are confining ourselves to sports-related study.

◆ City and Guilds courses offer, amongst other things, qualifications to work in sports centres.

◆ Business and Technician Education Council (BTEC) courses are aimed at people who want the option of going into higher education sports studies.

◆ National Vocation Qualification (NVQ) courses offer a practical, work-based type of study and are popular with those who are interested in working in tourism.

The above is a very simplified explanation of these courses and there is a significant amount of overlap and integration between them. You may take a qualification with one examining body, but have to transfer to a different one to achieve the final diploma that you require. For example, the BTEC First Diploma in Sports Studies qualifies you to go on to the General National Vocational Qualification (GNVQ) in Leisure and Tourism, as well as the BTEC National Diploma in Sports Studies.

All this can be very confusing and, in order to make it clearer, further details of these awards are given below.

City and Guilds
This is a vocationally based qualification with a small amount of academic content that can be studied at four different levels – Parts 1, 2, 3 and 4, with the last being the most academically demanding and hardest to pass. By comparison Part 1 is very practical and easier to pass. You

should not need any other qualifications to enrol on these courses although, especially if the demand is high, this may be at the discretion of your local college.

These awards are long established and recognised by all British-owned companies abroad. Many foreign companies also recognise them, but this will differ from country to country.

If you would like more information contact your local school, college, or the City and Guilds Institute (see Chapter 5). Their most popular course is Recreation and Leisure Studies so expect competition if you are applying for it.

BTEC

BTEC, which stands for the Business and Technician Education Council, concerns itself with numerous vocational qualifications including Leisure, Recreation and Management. These qualifications are recognised, in a similar fashion to City and Guilds, throughout Britain and by British owned companies abroad – although in Scotland they have their own version called SCOTVEC (Scottish Vocational Education Council).

BTEC has five levels of qualification ranging from Level One – the First Diploma or Certificate, up to Level Five – the Continuing Education Certificate (CEC). The BTEC First Diploma is equivalent to City and Guilds Part Two. The BTEC Level Three is equivalent to City and Guilds Part Four and also considered equivalent to the first year of a degree course.

No educational qualifications are normally required to enrol for a First Diploma level course. Most colleges accept candidates on the strength of their interview and references from their old school.

Further information can be obtained by contacting your local school, college, or the BTEC or SCOTVEC bodies or by reading some of the relevant books in Chapter 9. *A Guide to Jobs and Qualifications in Sport and Recreation* by John Potter/ILAM is particularly recommended.

NVQ/GNVQ

The National Vocational Qualification, and the SVQ in Scotland, were originally intended to replace the BTEC and the City and Guilds, and for a while there was a confusing overlap between them all. This appears to have been rectified to some extent by the examining boards specialising in different fields, so if your career choice was to work in tourism you would initially take an NVQ course.

The NVQ awards tend to be more practical 'hands on' courses, whereas you can take a more academic, theoretical level of award by enrolling on the GNVQ course.

More advanced awards

There are other, higher level qualifications offered in addition to those covered above, but you need to have some of the previously detailed qualifications before you can apply for them. You can get the information on these more advanced courses from your school, college or course tutor.

GAINING PROFESSIONAL QUALIFICATIONS

Once you have secured a job, promotion within it is often gained due to experience or attaining higher or professional qualifications. You could progress by gaining a Higher National Diploma, a Higher National Certificate, the Certificate of Management Studies (CMS), the ILAM Certificate of Leisure Operations, the Continuing Education Certificate (CEC), the ILAM Certificate of Leisure Management, the National Examination Board for Supervisory Management (NEBSM), university degree, postgraduate diploma, masters degree, doctorate, etc. The list continues to expand at a rapid pace every year.

Most employers have their own personnel department which will advise you on your own career development. If you need further advice read *A Guide to Jobs and Qualifications in Sport and Recreation* by John Potter/ILAM or other relevant books in the further reading section. You could also contact your local school, college, or career advisors.

ACQUIRING NATIONAL COACHING AWARDS

Many beginners level awards are quite easy to achieve, aren't too time-consuming and are also quite inexpensive.

For example the Level One Assistant Club Coach Course in Athletics lasts just one day and after this you are qualified to coach youngsters under the supervision of a club coach. There is no exam and the price for this in 2006 was £60 and that includes a manual of the course. If you wanted to be able to coach without the supervision then this takes a little longer and is obviously more demanding. It takes three days and costs £140. More details are available on www.ukathletics.net.

If you are interested in applying for a different coaching award, you should refer to the list of organisers in Chapter 5.

ADDING OTHER LESS FORMAL QUALIFICATIONS

Any qualification, no matter how insignificant you think it is, should be used to promote yourself to prospective employers. Many employers are just as impressed by applicants who hold other types of qualifications, as they reflect personal qualities not always found in academic or vocational awards.

Even just a swimming certificate or a typing course that you have passed could be useful. For example, if two people are applying for the same job, and both have the same academic qualifications to offer, then these little extras might just tip the scales to your advantage.

Don't forget if you are travelling, and intend to be changing jobs, carry these documents with you.

Some of the more useful ones, that should be noted on your application form or at an interview, are listed below. This is by no means a complete list. Gaining these simple qualifications not only opens up a multitude of job opportunities, but will also enhance your own lifestyle.

Driving licence
Many employers expect their employees to hold a current driving licence and, for insurance purposes, they often prefer the holder to be over 21 years old (in some cases over 25) and to have no convictions.

First aid

The basic first aid certificate is quite easy to pass and is highly valued by employers. They feel more at ease knowing that their staff are able to deal with accidents and emergencies.

Employment agencies often stipulate that candidates must possess first aid qualifications, whilst others particularly in the tourist industry are keen to advertise in their glossy brochures that all of their staff possess first aid certificates.

If you would like to take one of these awards, or would simply like more information look up the address and telephone number of your local Red Cross or St John Ambulance organisations on the internet or in the telephone directory. If you can't locate them by these methods, details of their head offices are in Chapter 5.

Life saving

Awards in life saving are absolutely essential if you are going to be involved with instructing or assisting with any watersports.

It is also looked on favourably by most other sports-oriented employers as it offers greater flexibility in the range of work that you are able to do for them. Even if you are only applying to hand out deckchairs on a beach, holding one of these awards will tip the scales in your favour during the interview.

If you would like to take this award then contact your local swimming baths for details. Their telephone number will be in your local directory. Alternatively, you can contact the head office of the Royal Life Saving Society, details of which are in Chapter 5.

Languages

If you intend to work abroad, speaking the local language has a most distinct advantage. Most positions of responsibility are advertised with this as a prerequisite for applying. Not all employers, however, ask for formal qualifications. They might ask merely for an ability to speak the language, in which case you can expect to be tested during the interview.

Even if you do not speak the language before applying all is not lost. Put an application in stating that you have a basic command of the language. Then start cramming up by using a phrase book and/or a computer or CD language course. If you are given an interview stress that you are willing to enrol at your local college on a language course, to improve. This will impress the interviewer that you are a conscientious prospective employee, and they will also realise that once you are living in the country your language skills will improve enormously in a relatively short time.

Other less formal qualifications

Almost any qualification is worth putting down on the application form or in your CV. Obviously these will be more useful if they relate directly to work that you are going to do. For example, you might not be a qualified mechanic, but if you have had a lifelong hobby of rebuilding old cars then your employer would probably consider this advantageous in someone who is applying for a driving job with their company and who may be able to fix minor faults immediately.

However, even if you think your qualification might not be relevant, still put it down as this just might help you to get the job. You never know, the company which is interviewing you for a job as a lifeguard in their swimming pool might also be looking for someone who has computer skills to help cope with the administrative aspects of the job.

LOOKING AFTER REFERENCES AND TESTIMONIALS

References are asked for by all employers and are provided by referees nominated by you. They are confidential and you rarely see them. Testimonials are 'open' references that you can get from someone in authority – teacher, youth worker, sports coach, etc – and are either included with your application, or are shown during the interview. If you have one of these in your possession it is vital that it is kept in good condition for future use. Remember, this is what impresses an employer and can often be the difference between being called for interview or having your application thrown in the bin.

SUMMARY

Qualifications

◆ Make sure your qualifications are suitable for the employment that you seek.

◆ Rectify any deficiencies by going on courses.

◆ Acquire the easier, less formal, qualifications like first aid. It just might tip the scales in your favour.

References and testimonials

◆ References and testimonials are very important. Get good ones and keep them safe and clean.

Language

◆ If you intend working abroad, start to learn the language and let prospective employers know this.

⑦

Securing the Job

MAKING THE INITIAL CONTACT

Once you have found a job or position that is of interest to you, your next task is to contact the person who advertised it. If you are applying to a big company it will probably have its own application form and you simply write a brief letter to the person named, asking for one. Examples of this type of letter and a company application form are given later in this chapter.

However, if you are writing to an employer or a smaller company which doesn't produce its own application form it would be advisable to use the following procedure.

Write to them personally and under no circumstances send them a standard, obviously duplicated, letter. Most employers would take this as a sign that you are not particularly interested in their job, but simply after any work that comes along, and that if you have put in so many applications that you needed to duplicate them you might already have employment by the time they reply.

Making the right impression

Figure 7 is an example of a letter to a small company, in this case based in France. If you are fluent in French write this letter in French to prove you have linguistic skills. You should also send them your curriculum vitae (CV),

11 Oxford Street
Uptown
Surrey UP2 4YU
Tel: 0198 765432

28 February 200X

Monsieur Didier St Jean
Manager, Hotel Belle Vue
Valmorel, France.

Monsieur,

I am interested in the position of chalet maid that you advertised in *Skiing World*.

As can see from the enclosed curriculum vitae, I am very experienced in domestic work for ski companies as this will be my fourth season. Three of these seasons were in Italy, however, so my command of the French language is basic. I can manage to make myself understood at the supermarket and around town. However before taking up any employment I will be enrolling on a French course to improve this. I anticipate that by the end of this winter I will be relatively fluent. After three seasons in Italy, I speak Italian quite fluently.

I am keen to work in France as I enjoy the French culture and one of my passions is skiing which I hope to do in my spare time.

I would be grateful if you would consider me for interview or advise me on the next stage of the application.

I look forward to hearing from you.

Yours faithfully,

Michelle Morrison

Michelle Morrison

Fig. 7. Sample letter to an individual or small company.

the names of referees and any testimonials that you have, and a recent photograph, even if they are not asked for. This shows you are organised and have nothing to hide. It also helps to jump the queue on other applicants who are later asked to supply these.

The initial contact is all about making the right impression, so here is some advice.

DO	DON'T
Write in the appropriate language when applying abroad, if you can.	Presume that people from other countries speak English. This is often interpreted as arrogance.
Produce your letter on a computer or word processor if possible.	Write it on paper that has been ripped out of a notepad or similar.
If you handwrite it make sure it is neat, clean and easily understood.	Write it in any colour other than black or blue. Some people will be greatly offended if it is written in red or green.
Write it formally. Address the recipient Dear Sir, Dear Madam, Dear Mr... or Dear Mrs...	Even if the advert includes their christian name, address them as Dear Tony or Dear Liz. This shows a lack of respect and the employer may presume that you could be disrespectful at work.

If you've addressed the recipient as Dear Mr Smith you finish the letter with 'Yours sincerely'. If you started with Dear Sir you finish the letter with 'Yours faithfully'.	Finish the letter with just 'Yours' or 'See you soon' or similar.
Print your name under the signature.	Just sign the letter. Your signature may look perfectly legible to you, but it can be unreadable to someone else. The recipient might therefore not know who to address the reply to, and consequently not bother.
Include all the information the application form asks for.	Presume there are some things that your prospective employer doesn't need to know. It may hinder your chances or make it appear that you are trying to hide something.

COMPOSING YOUR CV

A CV is simply a record of you: your achievements, leisure activities and employment.

You will see from the example later in this chapter that it is normally written in reverse order, starting with your most recent achievements and normally finishing at the date you started secondary education. If you have any difficulty composing your CV there are numerous books in the library dealing with this subject, or you can get advice from your local school, college, careers company, or job seekers club. A job seekers club is usually located at your local Jobcentre.

Getting the CV typed

If you don't own a typewriter, computer or word processor contact your local job seekers club, school, or college as they will probably be able to help you. They might also be able to supply you with numerous printouts or photocopies for reference. If this fails look in your local free paper for somebody advertising 'professional CVs produced' – or something similar. There are normally several of these. It is better to pay a few pounds to them, and create the right impression, than to lose the job. They will also make you multiple copies of your CV so that you have spares to use for other applications.

Compiling your CV

Take your time when compiling your CV. Prepare it thoroughly. Your success depends on it. Other applicants for the job may have inferior qualifications to you, but appear to be better because of a superior CV.

Don't tell lies in your CV, but experiment with ways of making a better impression. For example, look at the work experience of Jane in the sample CV in this chapter. Her first job was stacking shelves in a supermarket when they became low on stock. She could have called herself a shelf stacker, but stock control assistant sounds much better.

Other points to observe are:

- Don't make your CV too long. Two or three sides of A4 paper are sufficient. If yours runs to more than this you must edit it. A prospective employer doesn't want to wade through page after page of waffle.

- Produce it on good quality paper. It gives the recipient the impression that you have made a special effort and that their job is important to you.

- Don't send a photocopy of your CV, the quality of the paper will be poor. The print may also be grey rather than dark. The employer will get the impression that you have sent out scores of applications and their job is nothing special.

- Avoid technical jargon, the employer may not know what you mean.

- Avoid slang. He may understand what you mean – but will not be impressed.

Altering your CV

The example in Figure 8 is not the only way to construct a CV. You can alter the headings to suit your qualifications and experience. However most CVs generally follow this pattern.

If you do change this structure try several different formats and get a relative or friend to look it over. It must look neat, professional and contain all the vital information. It must also present you in the most favourable light possible.

Name:	Jane Jobseeker,
Address:	123 High Stret, Workborough, Wessex WE2 4UP
Tel:	01234 567890
Date of birth:	29 February 1988
Nationality:	British
Education:	2004–2006. Workborough Sixth Form College, Green Lane, Workborough. A Levels: English Language (B), Mathematics (C), French (C) 1999–2004 Wessex School, Early Road, Workborough. GCSEs: English Language (A), Mathematics (B), French (B), German (C), Science (C), Geography (C), History (C).
Work experience:	Cutprice Supermarket, Sept 2004 to present date. Friday evenings and weekends. Started as stock control assistant in 2004 and recently promoted to cashier
Interests:	Member of St John Ambulance Brigade. Competition standard at both basketball and horse riding.
Other information:	I hold current St John First Aid Certificate. I hold provisional driving licence - taking test in three weeks time. I am currently studying for the National Basketball Coaches Award.

Fig. 8. Sample CV.

FILLING IN THE APPLICATION FORM

Always complete the form in black or blue ink, unless it specifically states on the form that it should be typewritten. Always write in capital letters, again unless specified differently. Read the application form thoroughly before starting to fill it in. It is often better to write a draft copy first on scrap paper, correcting any mistakes and making any alterations on that rather than the form itself. An application form full of alterations and mistakes immediately gives the impression that your work is slapdash and you will almost undoubtedly lose the job.

In your excitement to apply for your dream job you may be tempted to mail the application as soon as possible. This often leads to things being missed off that you later realise would have been advantageous to include. Rushing also often leads to untidy writing and a badly constructed application. All of this can be easily avoided.

◆ First, deliberately take your time. One extra day delay will probably make no difference at all, but a shoddy application will.

◆ Secondly, before you write anything on the form, write it on another sheet of paper to see if it looks right. If in doubt, get someone else's opinion.

◆ Think of everything. Too much is better than too little. If it helps, refer back to Chapter 1.

◆ Double check! Make sure you've included all of your skills, qualifications and experience on the rough sheet before transferring it to the application form.

Don't forget that the employer will probably get many more applications than there are jobs available so before they draw up a shortlist they have to reduce this number. Don't give them any excuse to eliminate yours.

A specimen application for P.G.L. Ltd., is shown in Figure 9 and will give you an idea of what to expect.

SUPPLYING REFERENCES
This was covered in Chapters 1 and 6. Refer to those sections again if you need to.

However, please remember that the terms 'reference' and 'testimonial' often get confused so check exactly what your interviewer requires.

OBTAINING AN INTERVIEW
It is not unusual for it to take quite some time before you receive a reply to your job application. Don't worry about it. Remember that employers are very busy people and will have received many applications. If they are conscientious they will read every application before compiling a shortlist for interview. What may seem like weeks of waiting to you is probably much less. It always seems longer when you are anxious, but don't let this waiting time be wasted time.

Presume that you have been unsuccessful with this application and continue to look for other jobs. This not only makes the days go faster, but also prepares you for the worst. Imagine, though, the delight if you are wrong and a letter later arrives offering an interview!

 **APPLICATION FORM**

First read through the details and then complete all sections as fully as possible even if you have attached other information such as a CV. If you require assistance in completing this form, for example if you have a disability, please contact the PGL Recruitment Team who will be happy to help you. This will in no way be detrimental to your application.

➤ **PERSONAL DETAILS**

SURNAME

FORENAMES [underline used name]

Are you 18 or over?   Yes ❏ No ❏

DATE OF BIRTH [Optional, unless you are under 18 at the time of applying]

TITLE: MR/MISS/MRS/MS/OTHER:

➤ **ADDRESSES**

[at which you can be contacted between now and your given start date]

HOME BETWEEN THE DATES OF

ADDRESS

DAYTIME TEL [including STD Code]

EVENING TEL

MOBILE

EMAIL
If you would like to receive PGL's Recruitment E-news please tick ❏

TEMPORARY BETWEEN THE DATES OF

ADDRESS

DAYTIME TEL [including STD Code]

EVENING TEL

MOBILE

EMAIL

➤ **LEGAL ELIGIBILITY**

Under the Asylum and Immigration Act 1996, it is unlawful for PGL Travel Ltd to employ anyone who does not have permission to work in the UK or the country they are applying for. All successful staff will be required to produce proof of identification on arrival at centre, e.g. passport, work permit or other legal documentation.

NATIONALITY

DO YOU HOLD A VALID EU PASSPORT?   Yes ❏ No ❏

Passport Number: Expiry Date:

DO YOU HOLD A CURRENT WORK PERMIT/VISA?

Yes ❏ [please send a photocopy with your application]   No ❏

Are you in the process of applying for one?   Yes ❏ No ❏

PGL is unable to apply for a work visa/permit on your behalf.

➤ **AVAILABILITY**

Dates between which you are available for work [please give precise dates]. If you can give the widest choice of dates it will increase our ability to place you.

FROM   TO
Preference will be given to applicants able to start work between Jan-May.

Notice period required for current job, if applicable:

POSITIONS PREFERRED [For list of positions see PGL Recruitment brochure or www.pgl.co.uk/recruitment]. If you are unsure which roles suit you best, please leave blank and a Recruitment Officer will call you for a chat.

1ST CHOICE

2ND CHOICE

3RD CHOICE

PREFERRED LOCATION OR CENTRES
Leave blank if you do not have a preference

1ST CHOICE

2ND CHOICE

3RD CHOICE

GENERAL

Are you applying with a friend?   Yes ❏ No ❏

Friend's name

Will you accept the job without them?   Yes ❏ No ❏

Have you worked for PGL previously?   Yes ❏ No ❏

If Yes, what year?

Have you applied to work for PGL before?   Yes ❏ No ❏

If Yes, what year?

➤ **CONTACTING YOU**

What is the best time of day to call you if we wish to discuss your application?

Anytime ❏   8am - 1pm ❏   1pm - 5pm ❏   After 5pm ❏

Although some formal documents must be sent to you by post, please tick your preferred method of receiving communication from us:

By post ❏   By email ❏

www.pgl.co.uk/recruitment   recruitment@pgl.co.uk   00 44 (0) 870 401 44 11

Fig. 9. Sample application form.

➤ **ACADEMIC & VOCATIONAL QUALIFICATIONS**

PLEASE LIST ALL YOUR ACADEMIC AND VOCATIONAL
QUALIFICATIONS E.G. GCSE'S. COLLEGE COURSES ETC.

(Use additional sheet if required)

➤ **EMPLOYMENT**

PLEASE LIST YOUR EMPLOYMENT HISTORY UP TO A
MAXIMUM OF THE PAST 7 YEARS, INCLUDING VACATION
AND VOLUNTARY WORK. EXPLAIN ANY GAPS.

CURRENT EMPLOYMENT

COMPANY

DATES   from   to

JOB TITLE / MAIN DUTIES

REASON FOR LEAVING

COMPANY

DATES   from   to

JOB TITLE

REASON FOR LEAVING

COMPANY

DATES   from   to

JOB TITLE

REASON FOR LEAVING

COMPANY

DATES   from   to

JOB TITLE

REASON FOR LEAVING
(Use additional sheet if required)

➤ **DO YOU HOLD A FIRST AID CERTIFICATE?**

Yes ☐ No ☐   [If yes please enclose a photocopy]

DATE PASSED:

TYPE OF CERIFICATE, I.E. FAAW:

➤ **DO YOU HAVE A DRIVING LICENCE?**

If Yes, please enclose a photocopy.

Yes ☐   No ☐   DATE PASSED:

MANUAL ☐   AUTOMATIC ☐

DOES THE LICENCE HAVE ANY ENDORSEMENTS?

                              Yes ☐   No ☐
If Yes, please give **full details** on a separate sheet

DETAIL YOUR BREADTH OF DRIVING EXPERIENCE

DO YOU HAVE EXPERIENCE OF:

DRIVING MINIBUSES OR VANS   Yes ☐   No ☐

TOWING TRAILERS   Yes ☐   No ☐

DRIVING OVERSEAS   Yes ☐   No ☐

➤ **LANGUAGES**

	FLUENT	CONVERSATIONAL	BASIC
ENGLISH	☐	☐	☐
FRENCH	☐	☐	☐
SPANISH	☐	☐	☐
GERMAN	☐	☐	☐
ITALIAN	☐	☐	☐

HOW DID YOU ACQUIRE THIS LEVEL?

➤ **PASTORAL EXPERIENCE**

Please give details of your experience working /
volunteering with young people aged 7-17, your interests
and any positions of responsibility you have held:

(Use additional sheet if required)

Fig. 9. cont.

➤ EXPERIENCE AND QUALIFICATIONS

Please indicate your degree of competence by ticking the relevant column. Circle any of the listed qualifications that you hold and add any which are not listed. **Please send photocopies of your qualifications with this application.**

	BASIC	COMPETENT	QUALIFIED
■ DINGHY SAILING	❑	❑	❑

RYA Level Seamanship/4/5, AI, I, SI, other:

■ WINDSURFING	❑	❑	❑

RYA Level 2/3/4, Instructor Level A1/1/2/3, other:

Are you a member of the Royal Yachting Assoc.? Yes ❑ No ❑

Membership No.:

■ KAYAKING	❑	❑	❑

BCU 3 Star, 4 Star, Trainee Level 2 Coach, Level 2 Coach, Trainee Level 3 Coach, Level 3 Coach, other:

■ OPEN CANOEING (CANADIAN) ❑	❑	❑

BCU 3 Star, 4 Star, Trainee Level 2 Coach, Level 2 Coach, Trainee Level 3 Coach, Level 3 Coach, other:

■ SURF CANOEING	❑	❑	❑

BCU 3 Star, 4 Star, Trainee Level 2 Coach, Level 2 Coach,Trainee Level 3 Coach, Level 3 Coach, other:

Are you a member of the British Canoe Union? Yes ❑ No ❑

Membership No.:

■ SURFING	❑	❑	❑

BSA Level 1/2, other:

■ WHITE WATER RAFTING ❑	❑	❑

SRA Level 1/2/3, other:

■ RESCUE BOAT DRIVING ❑	❑	❑

RYA Powerboat Level 2, RYA Safety Boat Award, other:

■ LIFE SAVING	❑	❑	❑

RLSS Pool Lifeguard, RLSS Beach Lifeguard, other:

■ HILL WALKING / CLIMBING ❑	❑	❑

MLTB Summer Trained/Assessed, SPA Trained / Assessed other:

■ MOUNTAIN BIKING	❑	❑	❑

OTC, Other:

■ PONY TREKKING/HORSE RIDING ❑	❑

BHS Trek Leader, Prelim.Teacher, AI, WRTA Trek Header, Trek Escort, other:

■ SKIING	❑	❑	❑
■ SNOWBOARDING	❑	❑	❑

➤ HOSPITALITY & EXPERIENCE

Please give details of your catering, hospitality, administration, customer service or bar work experience.

[Use additional sheet if required]

➤ PRACTICAL EXPERIENCE

Please give details of your gardening, plumbing, DIY, electrical, carpentry, fibreglassing, maintenance or building experience.

[Use additional sheet if required]

Fig. 9. cont.

YOUR SUITABILITY

As positions at PGL centres are covered by the Rehabilitation of Offenders Act 1974 (Exceptions) Order 1975, employment will be subject to satisfactory clearance from the Criminal Records Bureau (CRB) and other agencies as used by PGL. CRB checks provide PGL with access to a range of different types of information about you, such as relevant information held on the Police National Computer; including any spent or unspent convictions, cautions, reprimands or warnings. Minor, irrelevant misdemeanours are unlikely to affect your application. All information will be treated sensitively and in confidence.

Please give any details on a separate sheet of any of the above that may appear on your CRB disclosure document.

If you have attached a separate sheet, please tick ☐

If you have any questions about your criminal record in relation to this application, please contact the PGL Recruitment Team on 0870 401 4411 in confidence.

BRIEFLY DESCRIBE YOUR PERSONALITY:

WHY DO YOU WANT TO WORK FOR PGL?

HOW DID YOU HEAR ABOUT PGL? PLEASE GIVE NAME OF WEBSITE, NEWSPAPER, MAGAZINE, FRIEND ETC.

ADDITIONAL INFORMATION

Do you require any specific assistance, equipment, support or adjustments to be made to enable you to live on centre and to carry out the position for which you have applied?

☐ Yes   ☐ No

If yes, please detail what assistance may be required:

(Use additional sheet if required)

REFERENCES

You **must** provide the name, address and tel/fax number of **three** people who we can contact for a confidential reference.

- These must ideally be people who you have been in contact with **during the last 2 years** and who can give a reference regarding your suitability, experience and skills for this type of work (e.g. coach, youth leader; former employers/teachers).
- **We will not accept references from friends, colleagues or neighbours.**
- We may contact referees immediately, so make sure that the addresses are current for the next few weeks (do not give college or school addresses during the holidays).

All job offers are subject to the receipt of satisfactory references. We cannot process your application unless you include 3 referees.

1. NAME

COMPANY

ADDRESS

TEL   FAX

EMAIL

WHAT IS THEIR RELATIONSHIP TO YOU?
EMPLOYER / LECTURER / TEACHER / OTHER (PLEASE STATE):

2. NAME

COMPANY

ADDRESS

TEL   FAX

EMAIL

WHAT IS THEIR RELATIONSHIP TO YOU?
EMPLOYER / LECTURER / TEACHER / OTHER (PLEASE STATE):

3. NAME

COMPANY

ADDRESS

TEL   FAX

EMAIL

WHAT IS THEIR RELATIONSHIP TO YOU?
EMPLOYER / LECTURER / TEACHER / OTHER (PLEASE STATE):

I certify that the information given in connection with this application is true and correct and that if offered employment by PGL, any material changes to the information supplied will be declared.

I have read the data protection section of this form and consent to the use of my personal information for PGL's administration, monitoring or marketing purposes.

Please include photocopies of certificates and driving licence. Ensure you fill out all parts of this form in full, even if you have enclosed other documentation such as a CV.

SIGNED   DATED

Please return to: PGL Recruitment Team, PGL Travel Ltd., Alton Court, Penyard Lane, Ross-on-Wye, Herefordshire, HR9 5GL, UK

www.pgl.co.uk/recruitment   recruitment@pgl.co.uk   00 44 (0) 870 401 44 11

Fig. 9. cont.

Throughout the time leading up to the interview you should still be applying for other jobs, because:

◆ you might not be offered the job after the interview;
◆ you might attend the interview and find that the job was not what you expected it to be;
◆ you might discover another job that you prefer.

Preparing for the interview

Once you are given an interview don't just sit back with a warm glow and presume that you have the job. There will be several other interviewees, and the person who succeeds will be the one who is most impressive at interview. The difference between all of them often comes down to *preparation.*

First, and this is most important, note the time, date and place in your diary, or somewhere where you cannot lose it or forget it.

Secondly, if it gives the name of the interviewer, make sure you know what sex they are and how to pronounce their name. If you are unsure about any of this you should phone their personal secretary and enquire. Don't be embarrassed. Explain that you are confirming your appointment and would like to check on a few facts. You will not be regarded as someone who is unsure or lacking in confidence, but rather somebody who is organised and likes to be thoroughly prepared.

Then, out of courtesy, write to thank them for offering you an interview, and confirm the time and date that you will be attending.

Research counts

Now the work begins that can be the difference between success and failure. If you have applied to a company the chances are that they will have sent you some literature about their operation. Read it thoroughly. Make notes about the things that are big advantages in the job, and also anything that you want to ask questions about. During the interview you will probably have the opportunity to use this information. You will therefore appear to be well prepared and concerned about the company that you are hoping to work for – Big Brownie Points!

If you are preparing to work for a smaller firm that doesn't forward this sort of literature they will be more difficult to research. Nevertheless, you should still try to find as much out about them as possible and the local reference library and internet are good places to start. You can find information on all limited companies through the internet by accessing the Companies House website. The reference library should also carry details of all local limited companies and all back issues of numerous newspapers including the regional daily. You can also use the technique that was suggested in the earlier chapters with regards to finding a job – that of talking to local people. This could be at the library, the local pub, newsagents, garage, anywhere.

The above techniques can also be used if applying to a sports club but extra information can also be gained by the following:

◆ Checking out performance details and other background information in a specialist sports magazine or local newspaper.

◆ Seeking out people who have played or worked for this club and talking to them. There should also be plenty of players who have played against them and who can give an alternative opinion.

Making notes

Don't assume that you can remember everything that you find out about this company. Make notes. You may think that you will find out only a small amount of information which will be easily remembered, and this might be true. However, if you find out more than you anticipated some of the earlier data may be forgotten, so write it down. This will also be useful to revise from later and could also be helpful in formulating questions to ask in the interview.

ATTENDING THE INTERVIEW OR SPORTS TRIAL

There are certain things that are of utmost importance when attending an interview or sports trial. Ignore them at your peril.

◆ Don't be late.
◆ Don't turn up on the wrong day.
◆ Do note the location of the interview.

If you are unsure how to get there either check in an A–Z of the area, or go to Google Maps on the internet. If still unsure, enquire about the travel directions with the secretary. This could be discussed at your initial contact with them, or it could be asked when confirming your interview. It would also be a good idea to ask about car parking. Many a candidate has been late for an interview, even though they arrived in plenty of time, because they couldn't find a parking spot. There is also a possibility of getting stuck in a one way system or roadworks, so ask about these as well and allow plenty of time.

These enquiries show excellent interview preparation and the secretary is bound to mention this to the boss.

Succeeding at the interview
When you eventually enter the interview a few essential points are worth observing:

1. Be smartly dressed. If you can't make the effort to look good at the interview it will be taken as a sign that you will not make the effort in the job and could also produce shoddy work.

2. Be polite. Even if the interviewer introduces himself as Bill Jones, still call him Mr Jones throughout the interview.

3. Address the interviewer(s) by name. If he hasn't introduced himself, it is a big plus point to say 'Good morning, you must be Mr Jones.'

4. Look interested and confident. When the interviewer talks to you, or you are replying, look them straight in the eye. If you are nervous and look at the floor, or out of the window, this may be taken as a sign of disinterest or that you lack the confidence that they require.

Asking questions

Details of an excellent book *How to Win at Job Hunting*, are given in Chapter 9. This book goes into great detail about the sort of questions you could ask and those that may be asked of you.

Asking questions at the end of the interview shows that you are still interested in the job – but don't overdo it. Remember the interviewers may be on a tight schedule. Only one or two questions are recommended.

A big mistake is to ask questions that have been covered in their literature or during the interview. Interviewers will get the impression that you have been inattentive. If there is something from either that you didn't understand, you can get away with these questions by stating 'there was one thing from the brochure (or interview) that I was unsure of . . .' In this way you have already acknowledged that you know it has already been covered.

Good questions to ask would be about the following.

◆ Training – especially if this is your first job.

◆ Colleagues – who your superiors and subordinates would be.

◆ Responsibilities – what you are responsible for and whether there are any foreseeable problems.

◆ Salary – not recommended, early in the interview, to ask about salary, holidays or hours of work, as these may seem all that you are interested in.

At the end though, if any of these haven't been covered, it is vital to ask these questions.

SUMMARY

◆ Take your time with your application letter – make it neat and formal.

◆ Fill in the application form in black or blue ink – neatly.

◆ Take your time with your CV – type it and don't omit anything.

◆ Keep all your references and testimonials neat and tidy – they are very valuable.

◆ When offered an interview – still apply for other jobs.

◆ Be early for your interview – dress smartly and be polite.

◆ Revise for your interview – make a note of the questions you want to ask.

8

Accepting the Offer and Making Arrangements

ACCEPTING THE OFFER

If things have gone to plan you will be reading this section after you have been offered employment. Now you will need to tidy up some loose ends. You can accept the offer verbally, but before signing anything make sure that you have been given a copy of your terms of employment.

Terms of employment

These should include a job description, salary, weekly hours, holiday arrangements, any training necessary for the job, overtime pay and other relevant arrangements. If you are working abroad the arrangements for National Insurance contributions (see later in this chapter) should also be addressed.

If any of this has not been given to you in writing you should ask for this when you verbally agree to take the job. If your job is abroad you should ask your employer whether they take care of visa arrangements, or whether it is your responsibility.

If you have cleared up all the above the company will probably have a formal contract for you to sign. If, however, they are a smaller company that doesn't issue

11 Oxford Street
Uptown
Surrey UP2 4YU
Tel: 0198 765432

10 April 200X

Monsieur Didier St Jean
Manager, Hotel Belle Vue
Valmorel
France

Cher Monsieur St Jean,

Thank you for offering me the position of chalet maid at your hotel.

I am very pleased to accept the position and I look forward to working with you in such a beautiful part of France.

One thing we didn't discuss, however, at the interview was my National Insurance contributions. I would be pleased if you could inform me of the arrangments for these.

Yours faithfully,

Michelle Morrison

Michelle Morrison

Fig. 10. Sample letter accepting employment.

one of these you may need to write a letter of acceptance (see Figure 10). This is a simple confirmation and a gesture of thanks which may include any further questions that have not been covered above, such as travel arrangements, etc.

TRAINING FOR THE JOB

If you have accepted employment from private individuals or a small company, it is highly likely that they will expect you to have already trained and qualified for this job. You should already have the experience necessary to execute all of the required tasks of this work. Refer back to Chapter 6 if necessary.

Alternatively, if you are due to work for a big company the majority of them conduct their own training courses so that everybody, even if already qualified, is inducted into their way of doing things. This training period is a good way of meeting your new employers, supervisors and colleagues, and also gives you a chance to get mistakes out of the way before being put into a pressure situation where it could be more embarrassing and expensive.

If you have been offered a job that doesn't give training and you are not confident enough to go straight into it, or maybe you are qualified but have had a long break from this type of work, then it may be a good idea to look for some relevant voluntary work before starting with your new employer.

COLLECTING THE NECESSARY DOCUMENTS

If you are British, and working in Britain, you can skip this section. If you plan to work abroad you will need some, or all, of the following documents before you can work legally in a foreign country.

Passport

Obtaining a passport for a British Citizen is fairly straightforward as long as you apply in plenty of time. This process has been made even easier with the opening of the Identity and Passport Service (IPS) on 1 April 2006, so that the majority of this transaction can be conducted online over the internet, simply type in www.passport. gov.uk. The IPS recommend that you apply at least one month before needing to use this passport, if this is your first one. You can fast track this process, down to as little as one week, but it will be more expensive and may involve travelling to your nearest passport office and waiting in a queue.

Passport Offices are located in Belfast, Durham, Glasgow, London, Liverpool, Newport and Peterborough. Enquiries can be made, and application forms obtained, from most main post offices, many travel agents, or by telephoning 0870 521 0410, or logging on to the above website.

Always keep your passport safe and make a note of its number and place of issue in case of difficulties or, more particularly, in case it is stolen or you lose it. It is also a good idea to make a photocopy, or a scan onto your computer's hard disk, of its main page at home before departure.

Obtaining visas and work permits

If your employment is in the European Union there is no

need to obtain a visa or work permit before starting work. For many other countries outside the EU you will need both to be able to work there. Obtaining these can be a very lengthy and difficult process, so start negotiating these as soon as possible after being offered the job.

If you are lucky your employer may take care of this for you. If you are not, however, you need to contact the consular section of the appropriate embassy as soon as possible. These are generally found in London and are quite easy to trace through *Yellow Pages* or your local library, or, of course, through the internet.

The consul of this embassy will then advise you of the procedure, which normally requires you to supply the following:

◆ your passport;
◆ your birth certificate;
◆ a medical certificate;
◆ your educational qualifications;
◆ two passport size photographs;
◆ your marriage certificate (if this is relevant).

TAKING MEDICAL PRECAUTIONS

If you are taking up a job in Britain you can miss this section, however if you are going to work abroad the following should be carefully noted, especially if you are going to work in a remote region.

Over recent years the health care in many countries has become as good as, or better than, that in Britain, but it can be costly to obtain. Not many have a 'free' health service like ours, so a few precautions are well worth taking before commencing employment abroad.

1. First, make sure you are fit for the job. If it is going to be strenuous, work out before you go. Also ensure you are medically fit.

2. Have all your check-ups before you go – dental, medical and optical.

3. If you wear glasses take a spare pair. If you use any other appliances, and a spare is out of the question, make sure you have the appliance serviced. In the case of battery driven aids, such as for hearing, make sure you take a spare battery.

4. Have a course of vaccinations. These can take some time so check with your GP early. Typhoid, for example, requires two injections, one month apart. You can normally find out from the embassy which vaccinations are required, but the Department of Health produces a leaflet on this which you can obtain from your local surgery. They also have extensive information on their website www.dh.gov.uk.

5. Take with you any medication that you would normally use in Britain. If on an extended visit, make sure you have enough to cover its duration. Also take a first aid box that might include as well as the usual plasters, antiseptic cream and paracetamol, things like:
   insect repellent;
   anti-malaria pills;
   travel sickness tablets;

anti-diarrhoea medication.
And don't forget (hopefully you'll need) suntan lotion.

6. If you are working in the European Economic Area (EEA) obtain a European Health Insurance Card (EHIC) which entitles you to reduced-cost, sometimes free, medical treatment. This replaces the old E111 certificate.

The EEA consists of the European Union (EU) countries plus Iceland, Liechtenstein and Norway. Switzerland applies the EHIC arrangements through an agreement with the EU. It must be stressed, however, that this provides for *emergency* treatment only. If you need to stay in hospital after the initial treatment you will have to pay for it, so it is well worth taking out insurance. This will normally be in an all-in policy which also covers you for loss of equipment, baggage, money passports, etc.

It must also be noted that you may have to pay for this emergency treatment whilst abroad and then reclaim the costs when you return to the UK. So take a credit card with you with an adequate upper credit limit available. In most cases you will not be able to reclaim the full amount, but you might be able to claim for the difference through your insurers. Check before taking out the policy.

COMPLYING WITH NATIONAL INSURANCE REQUIREMENTS

You need to know, before you leave, what the arrangements are for your National Insurance contributions. Your new employer should be able to tell you this. However, if they are not sure then they, or you, can obtain advice and information from your local Department of Work and Pensions (DWP) Office, or by accessing the website www.dwp.gov.uk. This is extremely important as these arrangements will ensure that you are covered, even if working abroad, for losing your job, falling ill and numerous other benefits.

TRAVELLING THERE

If you are working in the UK you should be able to plan your travel arrangements by discussing them with family and friends, or by contacting your local bus, train or flight operator.

If you are working abroad you might need to make special arrangements, but usually your employer will help you with these and the cost is regularly included as part of your contract.

If you do have to make your own arrangements, however, there are a few useful points to remember.

- Make your arrangements early. If you leave it late you might not be able to find discounted travel. Worse still, you might not be able to get there at all.

- Look for the most convenient and suitable way of getting to your destination – the cheapest is not always the best.

- Arrange travel insurance that covers you for cancellations, delays, loss of luggage, etc. Take advice from a travel agent or insurance broker if unsure. You can find a multitude of these by conducting a search on the internet.

SUMMARY

◆ Write a letter of acceptance. Use it as a chance to enquire about matters that you are not clear about – especially terms of employment.

◆ Train or prepare yourself for the job.

◆ Make early arrangements for passports, visas and work permits.

◆ Take out insurance. Make sure it covers everything.

◆ Ensure you are physically fit – get medical, optical and dental check-ups.

◆ Take a first aid case.

◆ Make travel arrangements early.

⑨

Useful Contact Information

In the last edition of this book the full postal address of most companies was given, but since then a minor revolution has occurred, and now many companies only give their internet address as this is their preferred mode of contact.

COMPANY INFORMATION

Airtours plc. (Now part of MyTravel group)

Backroads, 801 Cedar Street, Berkeley, California 94710-1800. www.backroads.com

BUNAC, www.bunac.org.uk

Camp America, www.campamerica.co.uk

Canvas Holidays, www.canvasholidays.co.uk

ClubMed, www.clubmedjobs.com

Cross-Cultural Solutions, Tower Point, 44 North Road, Brighton BN1 1YR. Tel: 0845 458 2781/2.
www. crossculturalsolutions.org

Crystal Holidays, TUI UK Ltd, Wigmore Place, Wigmore Lane, Luton LU2 9TN. www.crystalholidays.co.uk

Eurocamp, Hartford Manor, Greenbank Lane, Northwich CW8 1HW. Tel: 0870 9019 410. www.eurocamp.-co.uk

European Waterways, 35 Wharf Road, Wraysbury, Middlesex TW19 5JQ. Tel: (01784) 482439.
www.gobarging.com

First Choice, HR Direct, Jetset House, Lowfield Heath, Crawley RH11 OPQ. Tel: 0870 750 1204. www.firstchoice4jobs.co.uk

Halsbury Travel, 35 Churchill Park, Colwick Business Est, Notts NG4 2HF. Tel: (0115) 940 4303. www.halsbury.com

Ian Mearns Holidays, Tannery Yard, Witney St, Burford Oxon OX18 4DP. Tel: (01993) 822655. www.ianmearnsholidays.co.uk

Keycamp, Hartford Manor, Greenbank Lane, Northwich CW8 1HW. Tel: 0870 9019 410. www2.keycamp.co.uk

Mark Warner Ltd, 61–65 Kensington Church Street, London W8 4BA. Tel: 0870 033 0750. www.markwarner.co.uk

My Travel, www.overseasjobs@mytravel.co.uk

PGLTravel Ltd, Alton Court, Penyard Lane, Ross-on-Wye, Hereford HR9 5GL. Tel: 08700 551 551. www. pgl.co.uk

Ramblers Holidays, Lemsford Mill, Welwyn Garden City AL8 7TR. Tel: (01707) 331133. www.ramblersholidays.co.uk

Sunsail, The Port House, Port Solent, Portsmouth PO6 4TH. Tel: (023) 9222 2329. www.sunsail.co.uk

Travel Class Ltd., 14 Queensway, New Milton, Hants BH25 5NN. Tel: 0870 133773. www.travelclass.co.uk

VSO Voluntary Service Overseas, 317 Putney Bridge Road, London SW15 2PN. Tel: (020) 8780 7200. www.vso.org.uk

BOOK INFORMATION

Many of the following books have been used in researching *Working in Sport*. Most are available from the job section of public libraries, but if you run into difficulties it should be possible, with the information given, to order them from major book stores.

A Guide to Jobs and Qualifications in Sport And Recreation, John Potter/ILAM (John Potter Publications).

A Guide to Professional Sport, Various (The Institute of Professional Sport).

A Year Off . . . or A Year, Suzanne Straw (Hobson/CRAC).

Careers in Sport, Compendium (The Sports Council).

Careers in Sport, Louise Fyfe (Kogan Page).

Careers in Teaching, Ewan McLeish (Trotman).

Careers in the Travel Industry, C. Chester (Kogan Page).

Cruise Ship Job Guide, John Kenning (Harper Publications).

Getting A Job Abroad, Roger Jones (How To Books).

Getting A Job In Travel And Tourism, Mark Hempshell (How To Books).

How to Find Temporary Work Abroad, Nick Vandome (How To Books).

How to Travel Round the World, Nick Vandome (How To Books).

How to Win at Job Hunting, Ian Maitland (Century Business).

International Directory Of Voluntary Work, Editor David Woodworth (Vacation Work Pubs.).

Live and Work in France/Germany/Italy/Spain and Portugal, Vacation Work Publications.

Soccer Coach USA, Delta Publications.

Sports Scholarships and College Programs in the USA, Editor Ron Walker (Petersons).

Summer Jobs Abroad, Editor David Woodworth (Vacation Work Pubs.).

Summer Jobs USA, Petersons Guides (Vacation Work Pubs.).

Taking A Year Off, Val Butcher (Trotman).

USA College Soccer, Delta Publications.

Voluntary Agencies Directory, Various (NCVO Publications).

Volunteer Work, Central Bureau for Educational Visits and Exchanges.

Working Abroad, Susan Griffith (Kogan Page).

Working in Leisure, COIC (COIC).

Working in Ski Resorts, V. Pybus and C. James (Vacation Work Pubs.).

Yacht Crew Jobs, Delta Publications.

MAGAZINE AND NEWSPAPER INFORMATION

Anglers Mail, IPC Magazines, Kings Reach Tower, Stamford Street, London SE1 9LS

Angling Times, EMAP Publishing, Bretton Court, Peterborough PE3 8DZ

Athletics Weekly, EMAP Publishing, Bretton Court, Peterborough PE3 8DZ

Boat International, 5 Kingston Hill, Kingston on Thames, Surrey KT2 7PW

British Horse British Horse Society, Stoneleigh, Kenilworth CV8 2LR

Camping Magazine, Link House, Dingwall, Croydon CR9 2TA

Cycling Plus, Future Publishing, 30 Monmouth St, Bath BA1 2BW

Cycling World, Andrew House, 2a Granville Rd, Sidcup DA14 4BN

Equestrian Times, International Equestrian News Network, PO Box 227, Marshfield Hills, MA 02051 USA. Tel: +1 781 834-0550 www.equestriantimes.com

Footballers World, Newton Wells, 57 High St, Hampton TW12 2SX

FourFourTwo, The Magazine Group, PO Box 326, Sittingbourne Research Centre, Kent ME9 8PX. Tel: 0870 442 9513 www.magazine-group.co.uk

Golf Monthly, IPC Magazines, Kings Reach Tower, Stamford Street, London SE1 9LS

Golf Weekly, EMAP Publishing, Bretton Court, Peterborough PE3 8DZ

Golfer, The, Village Green Publishing, 24a Brook Mews North, Paddington, London W2 3BW

Good Ski Guide, The, 91 High Street, Esher, Surrey KT10 9QD

Hockey Digest, Unit E6, Aladdin Workspace, 426 Long Drive, Greenford, Middlesex UB6 8UH

Horse and Hound, Tel: (020) 7261 6315. www.horseandhound.co.uk

Jobsearch, www.jobsearch.co.uk

Martial Arts Today, HLL Publications Ltd, Greater London House, Hampstead, London NW1 7QQ

Mountain Biker International, United Leisure Magazines, PO Box 3205, 4 Selsdon Way, London E14 9GL

Northern Echo, PO Box 14, Priestgate, Darlington DL1 1NF

Overseas Jobs Express, Premier House, Shoreham Airport, West Sussex BN43 5FF www.overseasjobsexpress.co.uk

Rugby World, IPC Magazines, Kings Reach Tower, Stamford Street, London SE1 9LS

Sport Diver, Market Link Publishing, Ty Green Elsenham, Bishops Stortford CM22 6DY

Sports Boat and Waterski International, Brinkworth House, Chippenham SN15 5DF

Sports Quarterly, The Vinegar Factory, 20 Bowden Street, London SE11 4DS

Stage, The, 47 Bermondsey Street, London SE1 3XT. Fax: (020) 7357 9287. www.thestage.co.uk

Swimming Times, Harold Fern House, Derby Square, Loughborough LE11 0AL

Tennis Ace, LTA, Queens Club, London W14 9EG

Tennis World, Spendlove Centre, Enstone Rd, Charlbury OX7 3PQ

Total Fitness, 260 Great North Rd., Woodlands, Doncaster DN6 7HP

Windsurf, Blue Barn, Thew Lane, Wooton, Woodstock OX7 1HA

Working Traveller, The, Magazine for working abroad by payaway.co.uk

World Soccer, IPC Magazines, Kings Reach Tower, Stamford Street, London SE1 9LS

Yachting Monthly, IPC Magazines, Kings Reach Tower, Stamford Street, London SE1 9LS

Yachting World, IPC Magazines, Kings Reach Tower, Stamford Street, London SE1 9LS

Yachts & Yachting, 196 Eastern Esplanade, Southend, Sussex SS1 3AB

SPORTS EMPLOYMENT WEBSITE ADDRESSES

There is a multitude of websites on the internet advertising employment opportunities. Listed below are just a small number of them that have recently advertised work with a sporting bias.

totaljobs.com	jobsatask.com	workthing.com
reed.co.uk	jobsgroup.net	monster.co.uk
fish4jobs.co.uk	summerjobs.com	jobs.ac.uk
hotjobs.yahoo.com	jobsite.co.uk	righttoplay.com

WORK NOT DIRECTLY CONNECTED TO YOUR SPORT

There are also many overseas opportunities advertised in the following journals that are available from most leading newsagents or through your local reference library.

Entertainment – *Melody Maker, Record Mirror, The Stage, The White Book.*

General – *The Working Traveller, Overseas Jobs Express, JobSearch, The Lady, Nursing Times.*

Careers Europe is the UK National Resource Centre for International Careers Information. It provides resources to careers services, Connexions services and other information and advisory services throughout the UK.

Glossary

Abseilling A rock climbing term for descending a rock face, or any other near vertical structure, using only a rope and possibly a harness. The Royal Marines and SAS are often seen on the TV doing this at great speed.

Accessing A term often used in computing to denote entering a computer program. Most commonly used for gaining entry to internet websites.

Activity holidays Holidays during which the holiday-makers take part in one or more activities such as golf, tennis, windsurfing, etc.

Assistantship See Graduate Assistantship.

BASI British Association of Snowsports Instructors.

BMX The full title is bicycle moto cross. Participants race against each other on specially adapted bikes over rough terrain.

BTEC The abbreviation of Business and Technician Education Council. A body that administers many sports related courses and examinations. See Chapter 6.

BUNAC The abbreviation of British Universities North America Club. They have been arranging employment at summer camps in the USA and Canada since 1962. They now also arrange work in other countries like Australia, Ghana, Jamaica, Malta, New Zealand,

Spain and South Africa, but the latter is generally of the non-sports type.

Bursary See also scholarships. Bursaries tend to be small grants to students whereas scholarships are much bigger and can be awarded to cover a longer period of time.

BUSA The British Universities Sports Association. A body that administers student sport in Britain and can also advise on scholarships.

Camp counselling A job, mainly in summer camps, that entails looking after the needs of the younger participants on the course.

CCPR The Central Council for Physical Recreation. One of the oldest established sporting bodies in the United Kingdom.

City and Guilds Short for the City and Guilds London Institute. A body that administers many sports related courses and examinations. See Chapter 6.

CV The abbreviation of curriculum vitae. Literally meaning 'History of Life', also called a 'resumé', mainly in the United States, this is simply a record of your education, employment and interests. Generally asked for by prospective employers prior to drawing up a shortlist for interview.

Cybercafé A commercial enterprise found on the high streets of many major cities that offers clients access to the internet, for a small fee. See also internet café.

Dude ranches A thriving, vibrant holiday retreat in North America that gives guests a taste of the old Wild West (without too much discomfort).

Embassy In the UK most embassies are normally found in London, and are the British headquarters of friendly overseas countries. You need to contact them to arrange visas and work permits.

Gap year See year out.

GNVQ See Also NVQ. Abbreviation of the General National Vocational Qualification. This is awarded by many schools and colleges around Britain and many courses are sports based. More details in Chapter 6.

Graduate A person who holds a degree from a university or college.

Graduate Assistantship Normally abbreviated just to Assistantship. These are places given to graduates. They normally receive a grant to cover the cost of their studies for a higher level degree course in return for some teaching or coaching. Sports Assistantships are usually found in the USA.

ILAM An abbreviation of the Institute of Leisure and Amenity Management who administer their own internal examinations. See Chapter 6.

Internet The internet was developed in 1969 as a means of passing information from one computer to another. It has been refered to as 'the information superhighway' and it is a very fast way of accessing all kinds of information from all around the world.

Internet café A commercial enterprise found on the high streets of many major cities that offers clients access to the internet, for a small fee. See also cybercafé.

Leisure company One of a growing number of companies set up to cater for holidaymakers' needs. They normally arrange things from flights, accommodation, and currency, to sports courses and competitions.

NVQ See Also GNVQ. Abbreviation of the National Vocational Qualification. This is awarded by many schools and colleges around Britain and many courses are sports based. More details in Chapter 6.

Passport A formal document issued by the Passport Office (see Chapter 8). This entitles you to leave Britain for another country. There are seven Passport Offices around Britain and application can now be made online.

Prize money Money gained by winning or being placed in a tournament. A precarious way of earning a living. If you don't win you don't eat!

Professional In sporting terms, a person who makes a living out of sport.

Professional (golf) A golf pro makes a living out of coaching, organising tournaments and running a golf shop.

Professional (tournament) A golf tournament pro plays for a living and makes money out of being placed highly in tournaments, as well as receiving sponsorship and advertising revenue.

PTI Abbreviation of Physical Training Instructor. A position held in the Armed Forces (see Chapter 2).

References A record of your employment with an employer who normally sends them, on request, to a prospective employer.

Rep Abbreviated form of representative. This is a person who represents a holiday company or similar organisation and is employed to look after their clients.

Resumé See CV.

Scholarship Scholarships are grants that are often awarded to students who universities and colleges are keen to enrol. They vary in size from a couple of hundred pounds to thousands. See Chapter 3 for more details.

SCOTVEC Abbreviation of Scottish Vocational Education Council who administer the equivalent of the BTEC qualification in Scotland. See Chapter 6.

Semi-Pro A person who makes money through sport, but not enough to live on, so has another job to boost earnings.

Shortlist A list of candidates for a job that has been reduced from all applications, and normally the ones that have been selected for interview.

Sponsorship Funding given to sportspeople, mainly by commercial organisations, in return for the promotion of their product.

Sport England The National Governing Body for sport in England. See Chapter 5.

Sport Scotland The National Governing Body for sport in Scotland. See Chapter 5.

Sports Council The old name for the National Governing Body for sport in the UK. Replaced by Sports Councils for the individual countries: England, Ireland, Scotland and Wales.

Sports Council for Northern Ireland The National Governing Body for sport in Northern Ireland. See Chapter 5.

Sports Council for Wales The National Governing Body for sport in Wales. See Chapter 5.

Summer camp Originally an American concept but now growing in popularity around the world. These holiday camps are set up to usefully occupy schoolchildren during their long summer break. Courses range from arts and crafts to numerous sports.

Terms of employment A document that should be supplied

by an employer detailing the working practice and conditions for new employees.

Visa Many countries outside of the European Union require visitors to obtain an entry permit, or visa, for their country. These are normally acquired *before* travelling from their embassy, to allow immigration.

Voluntary work Historically this was unpaid work for a charitable organisation. Now some of this work carries a small salary – normally enough to cover all incurred expenses plus a little pocket money. Flights, accommodation, food and sometimes clothes are covered. See Chapter 3 for more details.

VSO An abbreviation of Voluntary Service Overseas. A long established reputable aid agency. See Chapter 3 for more details.

Work permit Many countries outside of the European Union require visitors to hold a work permit for their country before being allowed through immigration. These are normally acquired *before* travelling from their embassy.

Year out Taking a 'year out' or a 'gap year' is the term commonly used by students who either take a break from studies before going to university, or part way through their course, or after finishing and before taking up their chosen career.

References

1. *Focus on Sport*, Editor Craig Donnellan (Independence Educational Publishers, April 2006).
2. The Independent and the Professional Footballers' Association. 2006.
3. *The Times*.

Index